THE CHRISTIAN FAITH AND ITS SYMBOLS

JAN THOMPSON

Hodder & Stoughton

A MEMBER OF THE HODDER HEADLINE GROUP

ACKNOWLEDGEMENTS

Scriptures quoted from the NIV published by Hodder & Stoughton, © International Bible Society 1973, 1978, 1984, with permission.

The publishers would like to thank the following for permission to reproduce copyright illustrations in this volume:

Andes Press Agency p21, 23, 37, 40, 42, 66, 68, 71; Bridgeman Art Library p35, 72; The British Library p38; G. Graham p48; Sally and Richard Greenhill p61; Hutchison Library/John Fuller p74; Icon*Art*/E. Bakalarz p45; Impact/Homer Sykes p29; Judges of Hastings (01424 420919) p33; Life File/Emma Lee p64; Popperfoto p11; Religious Society of Friends p28; Trip/M. Feeney p55; Jan Thompson p15, 19, 34, 40, 41, 43, 51, 53, 61, 62; Mel Thompson p27, 50; Topham p15, 73; Rita Turner p64; Woodmansterne p24.

Every effort has been made to trace and acknowledge copyright. The publishers will be glad to make suitable arrangements with any copyright holders whom it has not been possible to contact.

Illustrated by Tom Cross Illustration

Orders: please contact Bookpoint Ltd, 130 Milton Park, Abingdon, Oxon OX14 4SB. Telephone: (44) 01235 827720, Fax: (44) 01235 400454. Lines are open from 9.00 – 6.00, Monday to Saturday, with a 24 hour message answering service. You can also visit our website www.hodderheadline.co.uk

Cataloguing in Publication Data is available from the British Library

ISBN 0 340 66379 0

First published 1996

Impression number   10 9 8 7 6 5

Year   2003 2002

Copyright © 1996 by Jan Thompson

Typesetting and design by Mind's Eve Design.

Printed in Hong Kong for Hodder & Stoughton Educational, a division of Hodder Headline Plc, 338 Euston Road, London NW1 3BH.

Contents

PREFACE

The Christian Faith and its Symbols has been used, and continues to be used, by many RE teachers and pupils since it was first published in 1979. With its concern to develop understanding of the symbolic nature of religious language, it makes an excellent introduction to Secondary School Religious Education. And for many new Agreed Syllabuses, its focus on Christianity is more topical now than when it was first written.

It was recognised, however, that it needed both a face-lift and some new emphases. When the book was first written, the aim of Religious Education tended to be to understand religion and its influences on the lives of believers. This may be termed *learning about* religion. With the more recent interest in spiritual development in school, there is now a growing concern that pupils should also *learn from* religion by reflecting on the relevance of religion to their own lives. Some new questions in the book have attempted to draw this out further. Others encourage a more investigative approach in places, and yet others make use of artefacts in problem-solving activities.

Despite these changes in this new edition, after the first chapter, the text has been kept as close as possible to the original to allow the old copies to continue to be used in schools where the new edition is also purchased.

RELIGIOUS **1** SYMBOLS

In this book you will be finding out what many Christians believe and how these beliefs affect the worship of the Christian Church throughout the year. None of this can be fully understood unless you first know what is meant by a symbol. As you work through each chapter you will begin to grasp how important symbolism is in religion. You probably take this for granted in other subjects like mathematics and geography. Before you can do any sums or read even the simplest map you need to learn the symbols used. This is also true of religion: you need to know its language if you are to understand it.

You will discover that symbolism affects the shape of a church building and the furniture inside. It affects the way people pray and the words they use. It affects the way they think about God and describe him to others. It affects the way people put across their religious ideas in paintings or music. It affects the colours, clothes and objects used in religious ceremonies and it affects the rituals, or actions, which are performed in religious services.

So let us check that you know what a symbol is.

SIGNS AND SYMBOLS

Symbols are like signs in that they both point beyond themselves. There is an old Chinese proverb which says:

> "When the finger points,
> only the fool looks at the finger."

Signs and symbols are like the pointing finger. You need to know what they are pointing to. You need to find out what they stand for.

But signs and symbols are not quite the same. Signs give simple information or instructions and their meaning is often quite obvious. How many of these signs do you understand?

Symbols, on the other hand, involve feelings as well. A flag stands for a country, but it also represents patriotic feelings towards that country.

Sally Gunnell was a British gold medal winner in the 1994 European Championships.

(a) Why do you think she ran a lap of honour with the Union Flag?

A sport's trophy *symbolises* victory. A certificate *shows* that you have reached a certain standard. A football scarf *represents* your loyalty to a particular football club. The colour red *stands for* danger. A scream may *express* terror. A scowl may be a *sign* of worry. All these are symbols because they stand for something beyond what they are in themselves.

Symbols may have many layers of meaning. A card in the shape of a key is a traditional symbol for an 18th or 21st birthday. But it represents more than the age of the person. It shows that they are considered to be adults by society, old enough to have their own home. The person whose birthday it is can look forward to new rights and responsibilities, but their feelings of excitement for the future may also be tinged with a little fear and uncertainty. And the parents who sent the card will probably have a mixture of feelings of pride and happiness, but also a sense of loss as their child reaches adulthood. All these different feelings may be summed up in that one symbol. After the birthday, the person will put it safely away somewhere. Years later, on finding it in a drawer or a case, it will bring back memories and stir up these deep feelings.

So symbols are more powerful than signs. They often express feelings which are difficult to put into everyday language.

ASSIGNMENTS

Use of symbols

1 What sorts of things are difficult for us to express in everyday language?

2 What other ways do people use to express themselves?

3 How could the following feelings be expressed without words: sadness, joy, hunger, fear, weariness and excitement? (You could think of other examples and mime them to the rest of the class to see if they can guess which feelings you are trying to portray.)

Symbolic actions

4 Discuss with a partner when the following actions should be understood symbolically:

clapping

waving

raising your hand

stamping your foot

patting someone on the back.

Symbolic objects

5 Think of something you have which is extra special to you. Why is it so special? How would you feel if it were stolen?

Symbolic clothes

6 If you have a school uniform, how did you feel when you wore it for the first time?

7(a) What do these badges tell us about the girl who wears them?

(b) Design your own badge to show something that you believe in.

RELIGIOUS SYMBOLS

We have seen why symbols are used generally. They are used in religion very often because they are the only way to express something. Religious language may speak about God, but Christians say that God is invisible and therefore cannot be described in an ordinary way. Christians have to use things which they can see to stand for God, if they want to talk about him.

For instance, when they call him 'Father', they do not mean that he is literally the man who fathered them, but that in many ways he is like a father and human beings are like his children. Christians call him 'Father' because they believe he created, cares for, protects, guides and loves all people, just as a good father does his children, only more so. He is not really a father, but this is used to represent him. 'Father' is used as a symbol for God and as long as we understand it in this way it can be very meaningful.

Christians use other symbols for God apart from 'Father'. Many of these can be found in their holy book, called the Bible. The following symbols are taken from the Book of Psalms with their references given in the brackets. God is called a shepherd (Psalm 23:1), king (24:8), light and salvation (27:1), rock (28:1), and so on.

The Lord is my shepherd, I shall not be
in want,
He makes me lie down in green
pastures,
he leads me beside quiet waters,
he restores my soul.
He guides me in the paths of righteousness
for his name's sake.

Symbols of Jesus Christ

Christians believe that God was known in the man Jesus, who lived in Palestine two thousand years ago. Therefore many of the symbols used for God in the first part of the Bible, the Old Testament, are also used for Jesus Christ in the other part of the Bible, the New Testament. There he is called Lord, Saviour, shepherd, light, bridegroom and judge.

In the New Testament book called Saint John's Gospel there are seven very clear symbols used for Christ. They are:

1   The Bread of Life

2   The Light of the World

3   The Door

4   The Good Shepherd

5   The Resurrection

6   The Way, the Truth and the Life

7   The Real Vine

Christians also made up symbols of Christ which they could draw or write down very quickly. These were particularly important in the first few hundred years of Christianity when they could not speak openly about their faith for fear of persecution. The fish was one of these symbols because each letter of the Greek word for 'fish' was the first letter of the words: 'Jesus Christ, God's Son, Saviour'. Early Christians drew this sign on the walls of catacombs, or underground tunnels, where they hid from Roman officials. Other Christians, coming across the sign, would draw in the eye, to show that they recognised its significance and to make their presence known to each other.

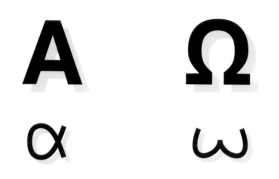

The first and last letters of the Greek alphabet, alpha and omega, were also used to symbolise Christ. This shows the Christian belief that Christ existed at the beginning of all things and will also be there at the end of the world.

'IHS' is another sign which is still used today and can often be seen on church altar-hangings. It is simply the first three letters of the word 'Jesus' when it is written in Greek capital letters. Greek is an important language in the history of Christianity because it was the language of the educated people at the time of Jesus and the New Testament was originally written in Greek.

The anchor was another symbol used by the early church. It forms the shape of a cross and therefore symbolised the death of Christ who was crucified. It also reminded Christians that their souls were anchored safely in Christ.

ASSIGNMENTS

8 Choose one of the symbols for God (eg. Father, rock). What does it tell us about what God is like?

9 Choose one of the symbols for Christ from Saint John's Gospel. What does this tell us about what Christ is like?

A SUMMARY

To understand religion we must understand what is meant by symbolism. It is not difficult because we are surrounded by symbols most of the time.

A symbol is something which stands for something else. Your name is a symbol because it stands for you. Your smile is a symbol because it stands for your happiness. When you put up your hand in class it symbolises that you want something or know the answer to a question. These are all symbols. They are not important in themselves but they are used to stand for something else.

Symbols are used a lot in religion particularly when people try to explain God. All human words were made up to describe earthly things and therefore they cannot be used directly to describe God who is thought to be superhuman.

So when people say that God is our Father, they are using this as a symbol to stand for God. They are saying that they think God is like the fathers that we know, only better. This is just one symbol for God. There are many others used by Christians.

CHURCHES

THE CHURCH

What does the word 'church' conjure up in your mind? Are you thinking of a building or people? Perhaps you are thinking of a typical church building with a tall spire, or with a tower rather like on a castle, surrounded by a graveyard.

But the church existed before such buildings were ever thought of. In fact *the church is not really a building but all Christian believers*. The first Christians did not have special buildings, they simply met in each other's houses. Some Christians today are going back to this idea by starting new churches in houses or halls.

Of course not all the Christians in the world, all 1,000 million of them, can meet together in one place. They gather together in local groups and this is why we speak of many churches. But these churches are the people in them rather than the buildings they use. The church buildings are best regarded as the headquarters of the Christian church or community.

ASSIGNMENTS

1 Copy out the definition of 'church' which is given in italics.

2 What does the illustration in this column tell you about the church?

What goes on inside church buildings?

Perhaps you have been inside a church building for a once-off occasion like a christening or a wedding. You may have attended a special annual service like a Christmas carol service, an Easter service or Harvest Festival. Christians also go to church for regular Sunday services and sometimes for weekday services too. Apart from worship, the buildings are also used for clubs of all sorts. Sometimes they are specially for church members, like choir rehearsals, Bible study classes and social clubs. These give Christians the chance to get to know each other better, to learn more about their faith and to take a more active part in the church community. Most churches also run clubs which anyone can join, such as youth clubs and old people's clubs.

Once you start looking into it you will probably be surprised at how many things go on inside church buildings. Sometimes the church hall is let out to other people to hold their own meetings or receptions there, or to run things like jumble sales.

Why people belong to the church

Now that you know what goes on inside church buildings you know many of the reasons why people go there and why people belong to the church. The main reason of course is because they are Christians and they believe that the church carries on the work which Jesus Christ started.

ASSIGNMENTS

3 Make a list of all the things members of your class or group have ever attended in church buildings.

4 Find some church members and ask them why they belong to the church.

5 Discuss with a partner what you belong to and how important it is to you.

Denominations

We can speak of 'the church' in the singular because all Christians belong to the same big group. Yet it is also understandable that they will divide themselves up into local groups, for practical reasons. It is like one big family of people who are all related to each other, but they cannot all live in one house.

There are other reasons too why Christians have split up into groups; some are to do with history and others to do with beliefs. You may know that some Christians call themselves Catholics, some Greek or Russian Orthodox, some Methodists and so on. They are all Christians but they belong to different groups, called

denominations. This is because the church, which comes from Jesus and his first followers in Jerusalem, split up as it grew bigger and spread around the world.

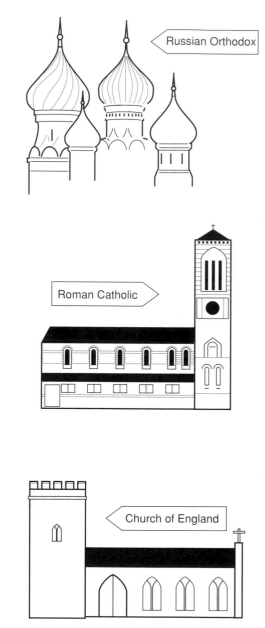

The Roman Catholic and Eastern Orthodox churches are the oldest and still preserve many very early traditions by passing on Christian beliefs and practices down through the ages. The Catholic church, led by the Pope in Rome, remained the only church in the West until about 450 years ago when some Christians protested against the wealth and power of the Pope. This led to the formation of the Protestant churches who ruled themselves: the Lutheran and Calvinist churches on the Continent, and the Presbyterian church in Scotland.

Soon the Church of England, or Anglican church, was formed when King Henry VIII also refused to accept the authority of the Pope, although this was more for political than religious reasons. Then more denominations sprang up in England like the Baptists, Congregationalists and Quakers. Later still, about two hundred years ago, an attempt to reform the Church of England led to the beginning of the Methodist church. These last four churches are known today as the Free Churches since they govern themselves, whereas the Church of England, being the established or state church, is officially ruled by the Queen and Parliament. More recently even more Christian groups have emerged like the Mormons, Jehovah's Witnesses and Christian Scientists. These are regarded with some suspicion by other Christians because many of their beliefs and practices are so different from their own.

ASSIGNMENTS

6 Would you have expected the church, which is nearly two thousand years old, to have developed in this way?

7 Think of as many reasons as possible why a person belongs to one denomination rather than another.

8 Do you think it would be better if there were no denominations but just one Christian church?

Ecumenism

In the second half of this century there have been several attempts to bring together again the different Christian denominations. In 1948 the World Council of Churches (W.C.C.) was formed. More than three hundred different churches belong to this from over a hundred countries, although it does not include the Roman Catholic church. This marked the beginning of the modern ecumenical movement. This strange word comes from the Greek for 'world', meaning the inhabited earth. So we are talking of a movement in the church to recognise that all Christians of the world are really united because they all belong to Christ's family. Many local churches from different denominations now get along much better and share together wherever possible. Each year many Churches throughout the world join together in the Week of Prayer for Christian Unity.

The badge of the World Council of Churches is the ancient Christian symbol of the ship, representing the church, afloat on the sea of the world. It is surrounded by the Greek word *oikoumene* meaning 'world'.

Design a new badge for the united churches.

There are important examples of this movement in the UK. In 1972 the United Reformed Church came into being by uniting the Congregational Church in England and Wales with the Presbyterian Church in England. The Orthodox, Catholic and Anglican Churches have also made greater efforts to understand each other. In 1966 an historic meeting took place in Rome between the Pope and the Archbishop of Canterbury. It was the first time these two Church leaders had met since the Church of England broke away from Rome. Then in 1982 the Pope visited England.

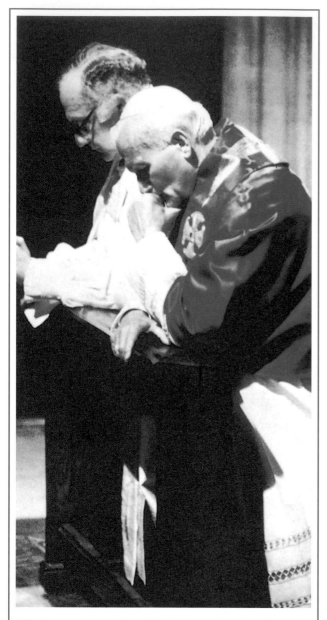

The Pope is the leader of the Roman Catholic Church, and the Archbishop of Canterbury is the leader of the Anglican Church. Here Pope John Paul II (in red) and Archbishop Robert Runcie pray together in Canterbury Cathedral in 1982. This was the first time a Pope had visited England since it broke away from the Roman Catholic Church over 450 years ago.

What do you think they are praying for?

Clergy and laity

Each Christian denomination has its own way of organising its church. However, they all have specially chosen leaders who usually work full-time for the church. They lead the services, make sure that the church activities run smoothly, and help the people to deepen their knowledge of God and the Christian religion. They are often called *clergy*. We can also call them ministers because they minister to, or serve, the people of their church or locality.

Their job may differ from one denomination to the next. In the oldest churches they are men who are ordained as priests and then remain so for the rest of their lives. In the Free Churches the congregations themselves have a say in who is going to lead them and they may only be appointed for a specific length of time. They may be men or women. Some clergy are more senior than others. For instance, the oldest churches have archbishops who are over the bishops who are in charge of the parish or local clergy. Because of the differences between the denominations the clergy go under many names. They may be called Father, Padre, Reverend, Vicar, Rector, Minister, Pastor, or just plain Tom, Dick or Harry, or Mrs Smith or Mr Jones.

The rest of the church can be called the *laity*, or *lay people*. This comes from *laos* the Greek word for 'people'. These are the ordinary members of the congregation: housewives, school children, babies, old people and people who go out to work. Although they have their own work to do as well, they often take an active part in running the church. It is surprising how much a lay person can do in his or her local church: he or she may be a member of various church committees which govern church affairs; a church warden who represents the congregation; a verger who keeps the church buildings in order; a sacristan who prepares the church building for services; a server who assists the priests; a sidesman who gives out the books and shows people to their seats; the organist and choir leader; a chorister; a Sunday school teacher; a club leader; a flower arranger and so on. There are other jobs also and some of those mentioned here may be called by other names in different churches.

These photographs show ordinary members of a congregation helping at a service. The two sideswomen are collecting in hymn books and service books. The server, dressed in white, is putting a cloth on the altar.

(a) As a class, think of all the things pupils do to help out in school.

(b) Why do they like to do it?

(c) Do you think it helps people to feel they belong if they get involved in this way?

ASSIGNMENTS

9 What is the difference between the clergy and the laity?

10 Try to interview a church minister to find out what training he or she had and what the work involves.

11 Discuss what leaders you have, and what makes a good leader.

12 What qualities do you have which would make *you* a good leader?

RELIGIOUS COSTUME

Sometimes you can tell what position a person holds in the church by the special clothes he or she wears. Scouts, Brownies and other such organisations have their own uniforms. Choir boys often look very angelic with their white surplices and white ruffs round their necks. Some of these costumes are traditional: that is, the same style has been passed down from one century to the next. The clothes which some priests wear for services were once worn by fashionable Roman citizens in the early centuries of the church. Some Protestant preachers wear a long black gown of the type worn in Geneva when Calvin started his branch of the church there four hundred years ago.

The Salvation Army Crest
* the central S is for Salvation; * the crossed swords for the fight against evil; * the cross for the Cross of Christ; * the 7 shots for the Gospel truths; * the surrounding sun for Jesus, the Sun of Righteousness; also for the fire and light of the Holy Spirit; * the crown for the crown of glory i.e. the reward God has promised to the faithful.

Some religious costume is worn, not just for its history, but because of its symbolic meaning. Many clergy wear a clerical collar, commonly called a 'dog collar'. This is meant to look like the iron halters which were fixed around the necks of slaves and by which they were chained together. In fact, a real dog's collar serves the same purpose: we can fix the lead to the collar and so have control over the dog. So by wearing this special collar the clergyman is showing that he is not his own master but his work is to serve God and be led by him.

Much religious costume is symbolic. It includes such things as 'one's Sunday best', the idea that one must dress up to go into God's presence. It would also mean considering why women often wear hats in church and why guards are posted at the doors of famous cathedrals to make sure the tourists are decently dressed. We shall concentrate on just three examples:

1   The Salvation Army

2   An Anglican bishop

3   A nun

The Salvation Army is a church which was set up in the last century by William Booth. It wants to save people's bodies as well as their souls and does a lot of good work amongst the poor and outcasts of society. The costume worn by its members looks just like a smart army uniform because the Salvation Army believes in order and discipline in fighting for what it believes to be right. They even call their members 'soldiers' and their leaders have officer's ranks. The colours of the costumes are also symbolic: blue trimmed with red and yellow. Blue stands for the purity of God the Father; red for the blood of Christ; and yellow for the fire of the Holy Spirit.

(a) How can you recognise the Salvation Army in this photograph?

(b) Try to interview a member of the Salvation Army to find out how they feel about their uniform.

(c) Why do you think they take their music out into public places?

(d) Do you think Salvation Army members are trusted by the public because they are so easily identified?

The Anglican bishop is dressed for a church ceremony. His hat is called a mitre and is supposed to look like two flames. This represents the Holy Spirit which is said to have come upon the first Christians in the appearance of 'tongues like flames of fire'. The bishop has authority to pass on the Holy Spirit when he lays his hands upon the heads of those who are being confirmed. Around his neck is the clerical collar. In one hand is his pastoral staff which looks like a shepherd's crook. This shows that he is in charge of a large group of Christians; just as a shepherd looks after his flock. On the middle finger of his right hand he wears a large ring. This is the sign of office, just as signet rings were used to give something the seal of authority. Other clergy will kiss the bishop's ring to show that they accept his authority. On his chest the bishop wears a large cross as a symbol of his Christian faith.

Now look at the picture of the Catholic nun. She is in traditional dress, although many nuns these days can hardly be distinguished by the clothes they wear. Her hair is covered by a heavy veil as a symbol of modesty; and her body is completely covered as a sign of decency. She wears plain, hard-wearing clothes: the clothes of a poor person with no extravagance shown. Around her waist is a rope-belt on which are tied three knots. These represent her three vows, or promises - of chastity, poverty and obedience. On her 'marriage' finger is a ring which shows that instead of being married to a husband, she is dedicated to God and his church. Around her neck hangs a cross which may also show which order of nuns she belongs to.

ASSIGNMENTS

13 Are there any clothes or uniforms which you wear because they stand for something?

14 Explain what is meant by 'Sunday best'. What do you think about people dressing up specially to go to church?

15 Copy the drawing of the bishop or the nun. Label everything they are wearing which is symbolic.

RELIGIOUS BUILDINGS

Church buildings have been designed to suit the activities which go on there. Some modern church buildings are used both for services and club meetings. So they may be simple rectangular halls with stackable chairs and an altar at one end which can be screened off when not in use. Other church buildings are more unusual shapes such as circular or hexagonal. In such buildings the altar, or Lord's table, can be placed in the centre and all the congregation can feel that they are really part of the service.

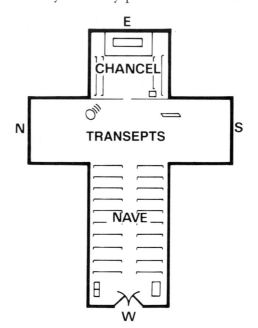

- It used to be the tradition to build churches in the shape of a cross. This is obviously symbolic, to represent the cross on which Christ died.

- There are other symbolic features too: the building faces east, towards the city of Jerusalem where Christ was killed and where Christianity began. To face east is also to face the rising sun. This is used by Christians as a symbol of Christ himself whom they call the Light of the World. One hymn to Christ says:

'Christ, whose glory fills the skies,
Christ the true, the only Light,
Sun of Righteousness, arise,
Triumph o'er the shades of night.'

- On entering such a church building your eye will be caught immediately by the high altar, raised up at the far end. This is given such prominence because these churches regard the Holy Communion, which is celebrated at the altar, as the most important service.

- Just inside the main entrance there will be a *font* which can be filled with water for baptism services. Its position by the door is symbolic because it shows that a person first enters into the Christian family through the waters of baptism.

This photograph shows a baby about to be baptised. The clergyman will sprinkle water from the font over the baby's head. The older established churches practise infant baptism (this is explained in chapter 9).

- Another symbolic feature may be the *lectern*, or reading desk. The one shown in the photograph is very ornate, in the shape of an eagle standing on a globe. The Bible is placed on the outstretched wings of the eagle. This represents the Word of God being carried all over the world.

- Another important feature is that the far end of the church, used by the priests, is often screened off in some way. In Orthodox churches this *screen* forms a complete barrier between the clergy and laity. It represents the particular holiness of that part of the building where the Holy Communion is celebrated.

Apart from these symbolic features, the traditional church building is also practical. At the far end there is the *Great West Door*, large enough for processions to come through it. Near the back or at the side there may be a *confession box* for people to speak privately to the priest and confess their sins to God. The main part of the church, called the *nave* is filled with pews or chairs to seat the congregation; it has an *aisle*, or gangway, down the middle. The *chancel* is where the clergy sit and from where they take the service: they may stand behind the altar set in an area called the *sanctuary*; kneel in their *stalls*; read from the lectern or preach from the *pulpit*. The *choir stalls* are also usually found in the chancel so that the choir can assist in leading the service, although some churches have an organ loft and choir gallery at the back.

So far we have been thinking particularly of the traditional church buildings belonging to the older denominations. The Free Churches have very different buildings. The first impression is that they are much plainer because they believe in worshipping God in simplicity. Often the main feature at the front is the pulpit, or preaching platform, rather than the Lord's table. This is because their main emphasis is upon preaching the Word of God rather than on the Holy Communion service. Baptists have a small floor space at the front of their buildings which covers a pool used for their baptisms by immersion. In the Salvation Army citadels there is a bench at the front where people sit when they are converted to Christianity. It is called the 'mercy seat' and symbolises their belief that those who turn to God will be forgiven.

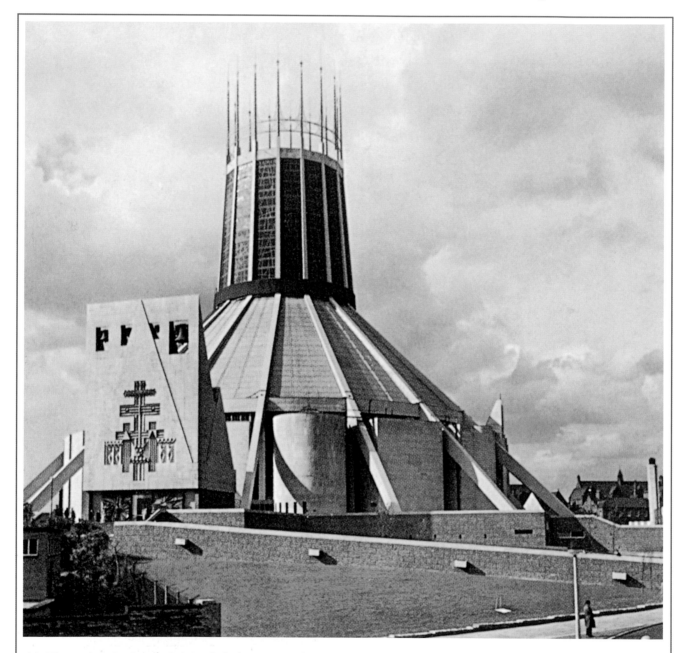

(a) This modern Roman Catholic cathedral in Liverpool is dedicated to Christ the King. How can you tell this from the design of the building?

(b) This church is built 'in the round.' What advantages are there for the worshippers to sit around the altar, rather than having it at one end? Do you think they would feel any different?

How important are church buildings?

You can tell from the number of church buildings that exist and the grandeur of many of them, that they are obviously very important to many people. Many church buildings are a national heritage: they are important historical monuments. Often they have been built, decorated, extended and restored with much skill, wealth and love over hundreds of years. Many are enormous buildings. They have absorbed the attention of masons, sculptors, painters, carpenters, metal-workers, wood-carvers, weavers and many other craftspeople and artists. They stand today as symbols of the faith and devotion of those who built them and those who still upkeep them. Some people like to think of their grandeur as a symbol of the glory of God; and of the tall church spires as fingers pointing people to heaven.

Although church buildings are useful and convenient, and often very beautiful and of historic interest, what would happen if a church building were closed down or destroyed? Sometimes this happens voluntarily: the church may decide that it no longer needs a particular building in which case it might sell it. In the past, church buildings have been taken over for all sorts of things, from factories to mosques. Sometimes churches are destroyed by fire. In such cases the church has to make other arrangements for places to hold their services and meetings.

ASSIGNMENTS

16 Copy out the diagram showing the plan of a traditional cross-shaped church building. Complete the labelling by writing in the following words in their correct places: Great West door; confession box; font; aisle; pews; lectern; pulpit; choir stalls; priest's stall; sanctuary and altar.

17 Find some pictures of beautiful church buildings. What do you think you would feel like inside such a building?

18 Why do you think some people prefer small, plain church buildings?

19 Do you think Christians are right to spend so much time and money on their buildings?

20 Where could Christians meet if their buildings were destroyed?

21 What would be the disadvantages of worshipping in a building which was not built for the purpose? Are there any advantages?

A SUMMARY

We may think of churches as buildings, but in fact a church is a group of Christians. As the church grew the Christians needed buildings. They meet in these buildings for all sorts of reasons but mainly to worship God.

The church has existed for nearly two thousand years and during this time it has split up into different groups or denominations. The main divisions are Orthodox, Catholic and Protestant. However, recently there has been more emphasis on the fact that all these Christian churches have a lot in common.

Churches are led by the clergy but the ordinary people, called the laity, can also help in many ways. Christians belong to churches for many reasons, but mainly because the Christian religion wants people to feel part of the big family led by Christ.

The church buildings are useful because they are carefully planned for all the things Christians do there. But even if there were no church buildings there would still be the Christian church. This is because the church consists basically of people, not buildings.

PRAYER

Prayer is a very important part of the Christian life. Christians pray together in church services, and privately at home. Many set aside special times for prayer such as first thing in the morning and last thing at night. These may be short sessions of about five minutes or as much as an hour or more. Monks, nuns and many clergy organise every day around their prayer times. For instance, the monks and nuns of the Benedictine Order have eight set services for prayer throughout the day and night.

Perhaps prayer can best be explained as getting to know God. It is not just talking to him but involves both speaking and listening. In the same way, if you want to deepen a friendship you cannot do all the talking yourself; both have to respond to each other. Nor do you need to talk to someone the whole time to get to know that person better. A lot of the time you may just be with each other, perhaps sitting quietly together, or maybe you express your feelings for each other in gestures like a friendly fight, a loving hug or by holding hands. To try to get to know God better, Christians sometimes speak actual words, out loud or in their head; or they may sing and dance, or just be thinking quietly, or remaining silent and open to God. All this is prayer.

ASSIGNMENTS

1 Copy out the following sentences, filling in the missing words:

People pray in order to get in touch with...

Prayer is both speaking and...

POSTURES FOR PRAYER

Because prayer is considered by Christians to be so important they have devised all sorts of things to help them to pray. For instance, there are special positions which they get into for prayer. These are usually both practical and symbolic.

- Some Christians stand for prayer. This keeps them alert; but it is also a sign of their respect for God, just as you would stand up to meet an important person.

- Other Christians kneel for prayer on cushions called 'kneelers' or 'hassocks'. Huddled up in this way, they can often concentrate more on their own thoughts; but it is also a symbol of humility because they are making themselves small before God.

- Less frequently, Christians prostrate themselves full length on the ground in prayer. This dramatic gesture is mainly symbolic: it is a position of extreme helplessness and therefore the worshipper is showing how much he or she depends upon God.

Some Christians do not use any symbolic poses. They simply stress the importance of sitting comfortably with eyes closed, and perhaps with hands together, so that they are not distracted by anything.

ASSIGNMENTS

2 Find yourself a partner who will get into one of the positions for prayer. Sketch him or her in outline only. Then colour in the shape in black to make a silhouette.

3 Try to explain the *symbolic* meaning of the position of prayer that you have drawn.

AIDS TO PRAYER

Some Christians, particularly Catholics, use prayer beads to help them to pray. These are called rosary beads. They are strings of beads which occupy the worshippers' hands and so give them something on which to concentrate. But more than this, each bead represents a particular prayer which helps the worshipper to think about the events in the life of Jesus and of Mary, his mother.

Another important aid to prayer is a prayer book. Most churches have service books of one kind or another. They contain the order of the various services they use and lists of Bible readings. In some churches the prayer book is very important and is used at every service. The Book of Common Prayer of the Church of England dates from the seventeenth century and until recently had to be used in Anglican churches by law. Now its services have been modernised. The Free Churches place less importance on set orders of service since they believe in having freedom to worship God as they feel fit. They prefer to pray extempore, that is, the prayer is unprepared and comes straight from the heart, rather than reading out a prayer from a book.

This is a collection of things which help Christians to pray. Make your own collection in school, considering how each item can be used by Christians when they pray.

Prayer is both speaking and listening to God. This shows a meeting of Quakers whose worship is mostly in silence.

(a) Are there times in the day when you are silent?
(b) Why do people value moments of silence?

WHAT CHRISTIANS PRAY

Christians believe that God is like a very best friend. Therefore they tell him anything and everything in prayer, and that is why Christian prayers are so varied. However to simplify things we can divide up their prayers into five types:

Confession

These are prayers in which a person owns up to things he or she has done wrong and says sorry to God for them. Christians believe that God is merciful and that all they need to do is turn to him for forgiveness. To 'repent' literally means to 'turn about'. Some Christians, especially Orthodox and Catholics, find it useful to confess their sins out loud to a priest. He can then help them to overcome their faults as well as assuring them of God's forgiveness. The 'Jesus Prayer' of the Eastern Orthodox Church is a prayer of confession: 'Jesus Christ, Son of God, have mercy on me, sinner that I am.'

ASSIGNMENTS

4 Why is it important to look honestly and critically at ourselves?

5 Can you think of a time you owned up to something you had done wrong? If so, describe how you felt afterwards.

Thanksgiving

Christians believe that God is the giver of all good things and therefore he deserves to be thanked. The Church of England has this prayer of general thanksgiving in its prayer book.

'Almighty God, Father of all mercies, we thine unworthy servants do give thee most humble and hearty thanks for all thy goodness and loving-kindness to us and to all men. We bless thee for our creation, preservation, and all the blessings of this life; but above all for thine inestimable love in the redemption of the world by our Lord Jesus Christ, for the means of grace, and for the hope of glory. And we beseech thee, give us that due sense of all thy mercies, that our hearts may be unfeignedly thankful, and that we show forth thy praise, not only with our lips, but in our lives; by giving up ourselves to thy service, and by walking before thee in holiness and righeousness all our days; through Jesus Christ our Lord, to whom with thee and the Holy Ghost be all honour and glory, world without end. Amen.'

ASSIGNMENTS

6 The General Thanksgiving is in very grand, seventeenth-century English. See if you can summarise what it says, in your own words.

7 Why is it important to say 'Thank you' to people generally?

Praise

People are praised for being good and for excellent work and behaviour. Christians believe that God is perfect and therefore he, above all others, is praiseworthy. In fact this is what worship means. Worship, or worth-ship, is the way people show their appreciation of God, of how much he is worth to them. When people praise God they are also caught up in a feeling of wonder at his greatness. You can see this in the following prayer of praise from the book of Revelation in the New Testament:

'Amen! Praise and glory and wisdom, thanksgiving and honour, power and might, be to our God for ever and ever! Amen.' (7:12)

Psalm 150 is also a prayer of praise, best sung to rousing music.

'O praise the Lord.
O praise God in his holy place,
praise him in the vault of heaven, the vault of his power;

praise him for his mighty works,
praise him for his immeasurable greatness.
Praise him with fanfares on the trumpet,
praise him upon lute and harp;
praise him with tambourines and dancing,
praise him with flute and strings;
praise him with the clash of cymbals,
praise him with triumphant cymbals;
let everything that has breath praise the Lord!
O praise the Lord!

ASSIGNMENTS

8 Choral reading is very effective with this psalm. If your class can be divided into ten groups, you can all begin by saying 'O praise the Lord' together; then group 1 reads the first line; groups 1 and 2 together read the next line; groups 1, 2 and 3 read the next, and so on. Everyone joins together in the last lines.

9 Find another hymn of praise and copy out at least one verse.

These Christians are praising God at a church service. *Why do you think they are standing and raising their hands to do this?*

Intercessions - prayers for others

Sometimes young children are taught by their parents to say prayers like this:

> 'God bless Mummy and Daddy, God bless Grandad, God bless Aunty Jean and Uncle David; God bless Snoopy my dog, God bless my friend Tom who is in hospital having his tonsils out and may he get better soon...Amen.'

There is a danger that this sort of thing can become merely a ritual along with the hot chocolate and bedtime story; but it does show us that Christians believe it is important to remember other people in their prayers, especially those in need. But does it do any good? Will Tom recover from his operation because he has been prayed for?

Of course, the very fact that someone is thought of at all is important because when we think of someone else, having their well-being at heart, we begin to see all sorts of ways in which we can help them. We become more sensitive to the needs of others instead of always thinking of ourselves. Christians believe that in praying for another, they are allowing God to use them for the good of that person. A famous prayer by Saint Theresa expresses this idea very well:

> 'Christ has no body now on earth but ours, no hands but ours, no feet but ours; ours are the eyes through which is to look out Christ's compassion to the world; ours are the feet with which he is to go about doing good; ours are the hands with which he is to bless men now.'

Many Christians believe that intercession does even more than this. They believe that prayer is a powerful and mysterious force. And what about Tom? Well everything that Christians ask in prayer is 'in Christ's Name', in other words, according to the will of Christ. They think that if it is God's will that Tom should get better then their prayers will help to achieve God's purpose.

Thinking of you and praying for you at this time.

Petitions - prayers for oneself

Petitions are asking-prayers, particularly when someone wants something for his or herself. If God is like a friend then it must be all right to ask him for things as well as giving him thanks and praise. True friendship involves both 'give and take'. But as has already been mentioned, Christians ask things 'in God's Name'. This is because they believe that God knows what is best for everyone and therefore they can do no better than simply asking that God's will be done, rather than trying to list what they think this should include, as children do for Father Christmas. When Christians ask in this way they are not disappointed when things do not turn out just as they had wanted; they still believe that God answers prayer, but in his own way. Even Jesus had to learn this: when he knew that death was very close he first asked God to let him escape it, but then he said:

> 'Yet not what I will, but what thou wilt.'
> (Mark: 14:36b.)

ASSIGNMENTS

10 Without writing anything, spend a few moments thinking on your own about prayer:

- Were you taught to pray as a child?

- Are there special times when you pray?

- Do you think prayer is helpful?

- Do you think prayer has any meaning if you do not believe in God?

11 Look at the card opposite. With a partner imagine a situation in which this might be sent. Who sends it? How does it make the person feel who receives it?

can be plotted on a map; but rather, it expresses the idea that God rules over people's lives. Lastly, talk of bread is symbolic. It stands for all of our needs, not just the recommended five slices of bread a day.

The Lord's Prayer

For Christians this is the most important prayer of all because it is the only prayer they have which Jesus himself taught his disciples to say. You can find it recorded in Saint Luke's Gospel at the beginning of chapter 11 and in Saint Matthew's Gospel in chapter 6 verse 9. The traditional English version, as found in the Book of Common Prayer, is as follows:

'Our Father which art in heaven,
Hallowed be thy Name,
Thy kingdom come,
Thy will be done, on earth as it is in heaven.
Give us this day our daily bread;
And forgive us our trespasses,
As we forgive those who trespass against us;
And lead us not into temptation,
But deliver us from evil.
For thine is the kingdom, the power and the glory,
For ever and ever. Amen.'

The language makes it difficult to understand immediately: there are several old-fashioned words which we no longer use, like 'art', 'hallowed', 'thy' and 'thine'. Even when you find out that these mean 'are', 'holy', 'your' and 'yours', the prayer is still difficult to understand because it has many symbolic ideas in it. We have already discussed the symbolism of calling God 'Father', and the fact that he is the heavenly Father, not to be confused with ordinary earthly fathers, is emphasised in the first line. Then to say that God's Name is holy is to say that God himself is holy, or set apart from people as someone special, because the name represents the person himself. The next symbol is in speaking of God's kingdom. Christians do not believe that this is an actual place where God lives and which

ASSIGNMENTS

12 In this short prayer most of the things people pray about are expressed: confession, praise and asking-prayers. Write out a line from the Lord's Prayer which expresses:

- being sorry for sins

- praise for God's greatness

- asking God for something.

A SUMMARY

Christians pray in order to talk and listen to God. They believe that in this way they can come to know God better for themselves. It is therefore thought to be very important and some Christians spend a lot of time in prayer.

When people pray they usually get into a special position. Some kneel down, others stand with their heads bowed, eyes closed and hands together. Positions like these help them to be still and also to show their respect for God.

They may use a prayer-book to pray from, especially if they are praying with other people so that they can all say the same words. There are other objects which help people to pray, like prayer beads.

Christians bring anything and everything to God in prayer. This includes saying sorry for their wrong doings and asking for his forgiveness. They praise God for his greatness and thank him for his goodness. They also ask him for help, both for other people and for themselves. The prayer they say most often however is the Lord's Prayer. It is called this because their Lord Jesus himself taught it to his followers.

THE CHURCH'S YEAR

THE CHRISTIAN CALENDAR

All Christians celebrate certain religious festivals. The high spots of the year are Christmas, Easter and Pentecost. The oldest churches, followed by the Church of England, have divided up the whole year into different religious seasons and festivals. They did this so that all the main events in the life of Jesus and the saints would be thought about at least once a year. The Protestant churches generally do not commemorate saints and therefore their calendars are far simpler. We shall be following the main events of the church's year.

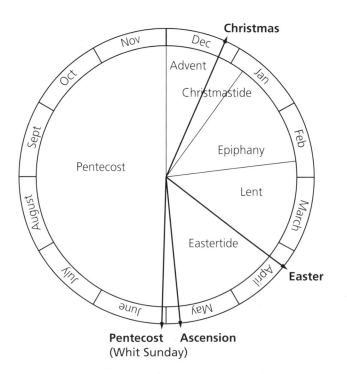

This year does not begin on 1 January but on the Sunday which is nearest to 30 November, Saint Andrew's day. The way the church divides up the year can be seen from the diagram, beginning with Advent.

The church has chosen special colours to symbolise each season of its year, just as we might say that green is a suitable colour to represent spring and orange for summer. During each religious season, any furnishings in the church building which can be easily removed, like the altar cover and some of the priest's costume, are changed to the appropriate colour. The church's colours are purple, white, green and red.

- Purple is a sad, sombre colour. Years ago people often wore purple at funerals instead of black. This colour is used by the church for the times of its year when Christians remember their own failings and their need for forgiveness: Advent and Lent.

- White is used for joyful festivals because it is pure and light: for Christmastide, Epiphany, Eastertide and Ascension.

- Green represents growth and it is therefore used for Pentecost, the longest period of the year, when Christians have time to grow in their faith.

- Red represents the blood of the martyrs, those who have died for their faith, and is therefore used for saints' days. It is also the colour of fire and is used to represent the fire of the Holy Spirit, at the festival of Pentecost or Whit Sunday (also called Whitsun).

ASSIGNMENTS

1 What colours would you use to represent Autumn and Winter? Explain why.

2 Copy out the diagram of the Christian calendar and colour in each section in its correct colour.

Here are some brief explanations of the different seasons of the Christian calendar. All of these will be explained much more fully later.

- Advent is a time of preparation for Christmas which celebrates the birth of Jesus Christ.

- Epiphany commemorates the showing forth of Jesus to the world.

- Lent is a time of preparation for Easter which celebrates Christ's death and resurrection.

- Ascension celebrates the withdrawal of Christ into heaven to reign with God in glory.

- Whitsun marks the coming of the Holy Spirit and the birth of the Church.

- Pentecost forms the rest of the year and is a time for Christians to deepen their faith in God the Father, Son and Holy Spirit.

- Saints' Days are times to remember the life and witness of particularly holy men and women who have been recognised as saints by the church.

SAINTS

ASSIGNMENTS

3 Find a dictionary of saints in the library and look up your own first names to see if you have the name of a saint. If you have, write down anything you can find out about him or her.

4 Write down the names of any churches in your area which are named after saints.

5 Find out if there are any towns, streets or schools in your area which are named after saints and write down some of them.

6 Are there any other things which are named after saints?

We all know the word saint; many things and places are named after them. It may even be that you are named after a saint. Yet it is a Christian term, so let us see how the church understands it.

The New Testament suggests that there is a sense in which every Christian is a saint. That does not mean they are all goody-goodies. The word *saint* means a *hallowed* or *holy person* and that means *someone who is set apart for God's work.*

When Saint Paul the missionary wrote to the early Christians he called them all saints. He believed that they were all called to lead their lives in God's way. His first letter to the Christians at Corinth in Greece says this:

> To the church of God which is at Corinth, to those sanctified in Christ Jesus, called to be saints...

A more modern translation says this:

> To the congregation of God's people at Corinth, dedicated to him in Christ Jesus, claimed by him as his own.

This shows us what Saint Paul meant when he called the Christians *saints.*

St Paul's Cathedral, London. Dedicated to St Paul.

Special saints

Because they believe that all Christians are saints, some churches refuse to name any special saints. The Free Churches have no saints' days.

The Anglican church, realising how difficult it would be to name every special Christian, simply sets aside days to remember those named in the New Testament, like Saint Peter and Saint Paul. It also celebrates All Saints' Day on 1 November to commemorate all the saints of the church whether known or unknown.

The Roman Catholic and Orthodox churches, being the oldest, remember very many saints and if you go into their church buildings you will see statues and icons (special sacred pictures) of the saints. When the church began, Christians wanted to remember the first leaders of the church and especially the early martyrs. As time went on the bishops of different areas kept their own lists of specially important Christians, or saints. By the twelfth century the Pope of Rome decided that he alone should have the right to say who should be considered a saint in the Roman Catholic church, otherwise the whole thing would have got out of hand.

The process by which someone is pronounced a saint is called canonisation. This literally means that their names are added to the canon, or list, of saints. This list is still revised in the Roman Catholic church. In 1969, several saints were withdrawn from the list, including Saint George, the patron saint of England, and Saint Christopher, the patron saint of travellers. This was because they have become too legendary in that there is now no historical proof of who these two Christians were, or even if they lived at all. Also, in 1976, the first Scottish saint was added to the canon. He is John Ogilvy who lived in the seventeenth century when many Catholics were persecuted for their faith. People still pray in his name and when a man recovered from cancer after such prayers had been offered for him, the Roman Catholic church took this as proof of his saintliness, although they usually require two miracles for this purpose.

These saints are usually represented in pictures as having a circle of light around their heads. This is called a nimbus or a halo. This sign was first used for the Greek gods and then the emperors. Christian artists took it over because it was a symbol of divinity and power and was therefore considered to be suitable for Jesus. By the fifth century it was also being used to portray angels, the Blessed Virgin Mary, and the saints generally. This was because they were all believed to be with God in glory.

This shows the icon-screen in a small Orthodox Church in the Norfolk village of Walsingham. Jesus and Mary take pride of place, surrounded by other saints.

(a) Who do you think the four saints are on the central doors (notice that each is writing a book)?

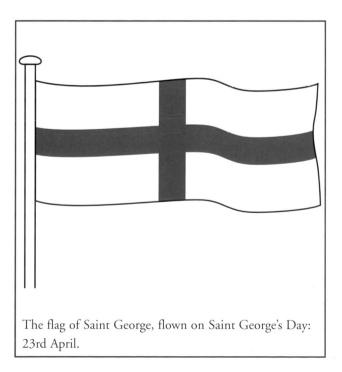

The flag of Saint George, flown on Saint George's Day: 23rd April.

(a) This is an artist's picture of Saint George. Of which country is he the patron saint?

(b) Find out all you can about Saint George.

(c) Explain why the Church no longer recognises him as a saint.

(d) Why do you think he is shown on a white horse?

(e) Why is he killing the dragon? (Notice that the dragon has a prisoner.)

(f) Why is the story obviously a legend and not historical fact?

(g) Does the legend teach anything important about good and evil?

(h) What 'dragons' (or evils) do good people have to fight in the world today?

(i) What sorts of things do you regard as saintly acts?

Why the church remembers saints

We have already seen that the Orthodox, Catholic and Anglican churches set aside many days each year to remember important saints. On these days part of the church building and the priests themselves are clothed in red, and the services are focused upon the saint who is being remembered. Appropriate biblical passages are read, especially if they are saints who appear in the New Testament, and they are thought about in the prayers. In some churches you will see candles burning before the saints, as a sign of reverence for them. The Christians who reverence the saints believe that they are now living in glory with God and therefore they can pray to them, asking them to assist with their prayers to God.

Saints are also remembered by calling people, churches and places after them. For instance, St Albans is the cathedral city where Alban, the first Christian martyr in England, was killed. If you were born in a traditionally Catholic country like France, or a traditionally Orthodox country like Greece, you would celebrate not just your birthday but also your name-day. Your name-day is the day of the saint after whom you were named. So if your name is Michael or Michelle your name-day would be 29 September which is Michaelmas, or Saint Michael's day.

The church has encouraged these people to be remembered because it is always good to use great people as an example to others. Each saint has his or her own particular lesson to teach. In addition, many of them were martyrs and this teaches Christians that they must be prepared to give up everything for the love of God, perhaps even life itself.

Most of all, saints assure Christians that it is possible to stand firm against evil and to defeat it. This is probably why Halloween is such a popular festival. It comes on 31 October, the evening before All Saints' Day, or All Hallows as it was called by the medieval church. By this time the autumn evenings are drawing in and it is the beginning of the darkest quarter of the year. This makes for a suitable setting for the ghosts, witches, hobgoblins, fairies and demons which are supposed to be roaming abroad that night. But as dawn breaks so the power of evil is broken, the bad spirits are dispersed, and the saints reign supreme.

A SUMMARY

Christians have worked out their own calendar so that they celebrate special festivals every year. The main ones are Christmas, Easter and Whitsun. There are also times to remember other events in the life of Jesus as well as important saints.

The word saint means a holy person, or someone who is set apart for God's use. Therefore all Christians could call themselves saints, if they cared to, because they believe God has called them to live their life for him, by following the example of Jesus Christ.

Nevertheless, the church does remember particular saints and puts 'St' before their names. The church has existed for nearly two thousand years and during this time there have been many special Christians who have been canonised, or recognised as saints. The different denominations have different ideas about which of these, if any, should be remembered on saints' days. Many Christians think it is important to hold up these saints as examples to themselves and others.

CHRISTMAS

ADVENT

Advent is a period of about three weeks which is set aside by the church to prepare for Christmas. The shops seem to get ready for Christmas earlier and earlier each year. Christmas has become very commercialised, that is, it is used for making money. Some Christians object to this because they say it hides the true meaning of Christmas. Others revel in the exciting atmosphere created by all the preparations for Christmas.

Christians use Advent to think about the meaning of the birth of Jesus Christ. For them it is the most important event in history. So this is a time for serious thought and prayer, represented by the sombre colour purple. Christians count off the days to Christmas, sometimes using an Advent calendar or Advent candle. An Advent calendar is made up of one big picture or a series of pictures which are originally covered up; each day one more piece of the picture is uncovered until Christmas Day itself when the whole thing is revealed. An Advent candle has numbers on its side so that it can be burnt down to a certain level each day until Christmas is reached.

Some churches also hold Advent Carol services, especially at colleges where the students will not be there for Christmas. These services have carols which are particularly appropriate to this time just before Christmas. A very famous Advent carol begins with the words 'O come, O come Emmanuel'. Emmanuel means 'God with us' and was one of the biblical titles given to Jesus.

This is an Advent ring. One small candle is lit in Church on the first Sunday of Advent, two on the second, and so on. On Christmas day they are all lit, including the large white central candle which represents Jesus the Light of the World.

(a) Design your own way of counting off the days or weeks of Advent.

ASSIGNMENTS

1 When is Advent?

2 Describe all the ways in which shops prepare for Christmas.

3 Make an illustrated chart to show all the things that your family does to prepare for Christmas or all the things that are done in school leading up to Christmas.

4 Do you think Christmas has become too commercialised? Explain your answer.

5 Find a copy of the carol 'O come, O come Emmanuel'. Copy out the chorus, and the verse which you think is most fitting for Advent.

The second coming of Christ

The word 'advent' means 'coming' and at this time Christians not only think of Christ's first coming as a baby at Bethlehem, but also of his promised second coming in his glory as God. Jesus predicted that he would return to judge the world. All the language he used to explain this was picture-language, or symbols. For example, Jesus said:

> Then they will see the Son of Man coming in the clouds (Mark 13:26)

> Keep awake, then, for you do not know when the master of the house is coming (Mark 13:35)

> When the Son of Man comes in his glory and all the angels with him, he will sit in state on his throne, with all the nations gathered before him. He will separate men into two groups, as a shepherd separates the sheep from the goats, and he will place the sheep on his right hand and the goats on his left (Matthew 25:31-33).

From the very beginning Christians have differed in their understanding of what this all meant. Which of these interpretations do you find the most convincing?

- Traditionally the church has understood Jesus as speaking of the end of the world when he would return in such glory that no one, this time, could doubt that he was God. Some Christians have even tried to predict when this would happen. There have been occasions when small groups of people have climbed up mountains to wait for the return of Christ because they were convinced that the end of the world was about to come.

- Others think that Christ has already fulfilled his prophecy of a second coming. They say he returned when he rose from the dead and convinced his disciples of his divinity. After all, he had said to them: 'A little while, and you will see me no more; again a little while, and you will see me.' (John 16:16)

Christ in Majesty from a Psalter of Westminster Abbey about AD 1200.

(a) How many symbols can you see? Try to find out what they mean.

(b) List the symbols for the four Evangelists or Gospel writers: Matthew, Mark, Luke and John.

- Other Christians think that Christ was referring to Whitsun, when he returned to his followers in the form of the Holy Spirit and continues to live among them in this way. On the first Christmas Christ came as a man who could only be in one place at a time. Christians believe that he has now returned to be with everyone at all times.

- Lastly, some Christians think that Christ's second coming does not refer to a single historical event at all. They believe that Christ returns all the time to individuals in a very personal way when they allow him to influence their lives. There is a Christian chorus with the words 'Come into my heart, Lord Jesus'. This expresses, in a symbolic way, the idea that there is an advent, or coming, of Christ to individual Christians.

LIGHT

Light and darkness are such powerful symbols that they can stir up deep feelings within us. We automatically choose light to express good things and darkness for evil things. We speak of 'a ray of hope' but 'shadows of despair'. Here are some experiences to do with light and darkness. Read them through, imagining how you might feel in each situation:

a) You get up very early to see the sunrise.

b) You wake up to see bright streaks of light filtering through your curtains.

c) You travel into the city on a dark evening where all the streets and shops are ablaze with lights and neon signs.

d) You watch a firework display.

e) You wake up alone in the middle of the night.

f) You feel the relief of sundown after a very hot day.

g) You watch a war film where the prisoners are trying to escape the searchlight.

h) You turn off the lights in order to go to sleep.

ASSIGNMENTS

6 Choose one of the examples above and either write a paragraph, or draw a picture, to express your feelings about it.

7 Can you think of any other experiences to do with light or darkness.

8 Try to write down some more symbolic sayings to do with light and darkness, like 'a ray of hope'. (It may help to think of the symbolic way in which the verb 'to enlighten' is used.)

9 Consider these words of a popsong by Asward:

Shine, shine like a star,
Shine so bright
like the star that you are.
Shine into the future,
spreading your light
wherever you are.

How can we 'shine like a star'?

10 Do you know any other songs which use the symbol of light?

11 A father said of his dead daughter 'she was a shining light.' What do you think he meant by that?

12 Is there anyone you could describe as 'the light of my life'? If so, explain why.

You already know that one of the symbols used to describe Jesus in Saint John's Gospel is 'the Light of the World'. This symbolism is used a lot during Advent because it sums up both the comforting and frightening aspects of Christ's coming. Light is usually a great help and pleasure to us; it brightens up our lives. Yet it does show up everything for what it is: nothing can hide in a bright light. Also the brighter the light, the darker the shadow that it casts. These good and bad aspects of light represent both the salvation and the judgement that Christians connect with the coming of Christ. They believe that Christ came to save humanity by lighting its way to God. But they also believe that Christ's light exposes all the nasty things about themselves which people would prefer to stay hidden. It is very painful to face the truth about ourselves and many people would rather skulk in the dark. This symbolism is very clear in the 'collect' or prayer for the first Sunday in Advent from the Book of Common Prayer:

'Almighty God, give us grace that we may cast away the works of darkness, and put upon us the armour of light, now in the time of this mortal life, in which thy Son Jesus Christ came to visit us in great humility; that in the last day, when he shall come again in his glorious Majesty, to judge both the quick and the dead, we may rise to the life immortal; through him who liveth and reigneth with thee and the Holy Ghost, now and ever. Amen'

(a) How can you tell that this picture was taken near Christmas?

(b) Why do we often use lights to celebrate happy events like Christmas?

ASSIGNMENTS

13 Think about the following things and then list them in two columns, one headed 'Works of darkness' and the other 'Works of light': forgiveness, kindness, evil thoughts, spiteful gossip, gentleness, bad temper, patience, bad language, telling lies, and humility. Try to think of two more examples to add to each column.

14 Why do you think light is described as 'armour' in the prayer on the previous page?

Not only is light used as a symbol during Advent but it is also a very important symbol at Christmas. One of the most popular motifs on Christmas cards is a candle; shops are lit up specially for Christmas; Christmas trees are decorated with fairy-lights and dazzling tinsel.

Inside church buildings you may see a Christmas crib. This is a model showing the scene of Jesus' birth. Usually they are lit up in some way, with halos of light around the heads of Jesus and his mother Mary, and a star hanging over the whole scene.

CHRISTMAS

Many churches have Midnight Mass on Christmas Eve when the building may be entirely lit by candles. This is a joyful Christmas service of Holy Communion, usually starting at 11.30pm and continuing into Christmas Day.

Light is an important Christmas symbol because it is the time when Christians celebrate the birth of Jesus whom they call 'the Light of the World'. But in fact, even before Christianity existed, 25 December was the midwinter festival of sun worship. At this darkest time of year we all feel the need to cheer ourselves up and remind ourselves that summer is going to come round again. If you watch the television advertisements at Christmas time you will see that they have already started to advertise summer holidays. Since the precise date of Jesus' birth was never recorded, Christians deliberately chose this date to celebrate Christ's birth. It seemed so appropriate at this time of darkness to remind themselves of their belief that God had sent them someone who could lead them out of the darkness of sin and despair into the light of goodness, joy and hope.

As you all know, Christmas is the celebration of the birth of Jesus Christ. The story of his birth is recorded in two books of the New Testament, the Gospels according to Saint Matthew and Saint Luke. The word 'gospel' means 'good news' and there are four New Testament books in which Christian writers have recorded the good news about Jesus' life and death. Saint Luke's Gospel tells us more about the actual birth of Jesus, while Saint Matthew's version concerns the later visit of the wise men which the church connects with the feast of Epiphany on the twelfth day of Christmas.

You can read Luke's story in Saint Luke's Gospel chapter 2. It tells how Mary and Joseph had to leave their home in Nazareth in northern Palestine to be registered in Bethlehem, a little town near the capital city of Jerusalem in the south. When they arrived, they had to stay in a stable because all the hotel rooms had been taken. Mary was pregnant at the time and whilst there she gave birth to her first child. It was a boy and they called him 'Jesus' which means 'God saves'. Christians believe that Mary was inspired to give her son this very appropriate name. The story goes on:

'Now in the same district there were shepherds out in the fields, keeping watch through the night over their flock, when suddenly there stood before them an angel of the Lord, and the splendour of the Lord shone round them. They were terror-stricken, but the angel said, "Do not be afraid; I have good news for you; there is great joy coming to the whole people. Today in the city of David a deliverer has been born to you - the Messiah, the Lord. And this is your sign: you will find a baby lying wrapped in his swaddling clothes, in a manger." All at once there was with the angel a great company of the heavenly host, singing the praises of God:
"Glory to God in highest heaven, and on earth his peace for men on whom his favour rests."
(Luke 2:8-14)

The shepherds took the message to heart for they had been told that the long-awaited saviour had at last been sent by God. They went and found the baby, telling Mary and Joseph what had happened to them. Then they left, glorifying and praising God.

We do not know how Luke knew this story. Perhaps he heard it from Mary herself, or perhaps it is one of those legends which so naturally grow up around great men and women. Some Christians believe it happened just as it says. Other Christians will doubt the history behind it but say that the story nevertheless contains truth because it says a lot of things about Jesus which they believe are true. For instance, in the story Jesus was born in a stable and laid in the cattle's feeding trough. This shows Christians that Jesus understood what it was like to be homeless and to have to make the best of things. They believe that he still understands the difficulties of the poor. Then the good news of Jesus' birth was brought first of all to just ordinary shepherds.

This tells Christians that Jesus came for everyone and that you do not have to be someone special to be important to him. The magnificent scene with the angels expresses the Christian belief that Jesus was sent by God and that it was all part of a heavenly plan to bring peace and salvation to men and women. So, whether Jesus was born in quite this way or not, the story is symbolic. The birth in a stable, the angel's message and the presence of the shepherds all represent important Christian ideas about the meaning of Jesus.

Christians go back to the story of Jesus' birth in order to understand the real meaning of Christmas today.

- It teaches them that Christmas should be a time for thinking about the less fortunate people in the world, particularly the homeless. Many churches make a special effort to give money to charity at this time and some go carol singing to collect money from others. Some churches organise Christmas dinners for people in their area who would otherwise be alone; and some provide shelter and food for the homeless.

- Christmas is also a time of great joy and the Christmas services and parties are very jolly occasions.

- Christmas is a time for family gatherings, and in many homes the celebrations centre particularly on the children. Christians would say that this too comes from the Christmas story since it is a time to remember the Holy Family at Bethlehem and the joy surrounding the newborn child.

ASSIGNMENTS

15 Write out in your own words the story of Jesus' birth, or draw it in a picture-strip.

16 What are the symbols in the story?

17 Collect together some Christmas cards and try to say what Christmas idea each of them is putting across. (For example: some will have biblical scenes on them, telling the story of Jesus' birth; some will have churches on them to show that this is basically a religious festival; some will have scenes of celebration to show that this is a time of rejoicing. You will find that some pictures on Christmas cards have very little to do with Christmas at all!)

18 Design your own Christmas card to put across a specifically Christmas message. Write a verse inside the card on the same idea.

Carol singing for Christian Aid in Trafalgar Square.

RELIGIOUS ART

Many people find it easier to express themselves through some form of artwork than in words. Ask a four-year-old who is having a temper tantrum to explain his or her feelings and the child would be completely at a loss. But give him or her a brush, paints and paper and the child would be able to express those feelings admirably. Some of you, given the choice, would always prefer to draw a picture than write a composition. Others of you may have lost confidence in your artistic ability and your illustrations may seem a big embarrassment to you. Artists go on to develop this ability and find that they can say things in shapes and colours that they could never put fully into words.

Art has always been very important in religion because we have already discovered that many religious ideas are difficult to put into words. People have found that they can use ordinary, earthly words to describe what is so much greater than the normal things around them. Some people believe in God as a real person yet they say he has not got a body like you and me, and he does not live in a place. They believe he is far, far greater than any human being and that no human words are great enough to describe God unless they are used symbolically. They use words like 'Father' and 'King' to describe God because these symbols point them in the right direction. But artists are not limited to words; they can express themselves in many other ways.

ASSIGNMENTS

19 Find a piece of music which lasts for about five minutes and listen to it carefully. Now take a piece of paper and something to draw with. Put the music on again and, once it starts, keep your pencil on the paper and keep it moving. Try to express the sounds you are hearing in the continual shapes that you make on the paper.

As we have been thinking of Christmas let us consider how the Nativity, the birth of Jesus, is expressed in art. The two most important people to be portrayed are Jesus and Mary. Mary, as the woman chosen to be the mother of Jesus, naturally holds a place of special importance in Christianity. The Orthodox and Catholic churches, particularly, treat her with great reverence.

This is a famous statue of Mary with Jesus, from the pilgrimage centre of Walsingham in Norfolk.

(a) List all the symbols you can see in this statue, and try to explain their meanings.

In Catholic church buildings there are statues of Mary. These are usually found in the Lady Chapel, a small chapel dedicated to the Blessed Virgin Mary, to the east of the High Altar. Many of these statues show her dressed in a blue robe and with a lily. Both of these things are symbols of her purity because Christians believe she must have been a very good and holy person to be chosen to have Jesus. Blue is also the colour of the sky, because Mary is known as 'Queen of Heaven'.

If you look at paintings of the Nativity in art galleries you will find that they put across various ideas about Jesus and Mary:

- Some pictures show lots of angels either adoring Jesus or dancing for joy in the sky above. The artists are not suggesting that we could have seen all this if we had been there. They are expressing the idea that this birth was no commonplace event but had far-reaching importance.

- Some paintings make no attempt to imagine what the houses in Palestine would have looked like when Jesus was born. Instead they use a setting from their own day and age, and dress Mary in sumptuous clothes that the rich women wore in their time. Again these artists are not trying to show what it was really like; they are showing Mary's importance in ways that people of their own day would understand.

Madonna and Child by Simon Vouet

- Other artists have tried to portray Jesus and Mary as they might really have been. Jesus is shown as a tiny, helpless baby and Mary protects him with a mother's loving care. These artists are trying to show that both Jesus and Mary were real people after all, and although Christians believe that Jesus was God, they also believe he was a real man.

- Sometimes Mary is shown worshipping her child. This puts across the idea that, from the very beginning, Jesus was far greater even than his mother. There may also be other adults kneeling before him.

ASSIGNMENTS

20 Find as many Christmas cards as possible which show the Nativity scene. See which of your pictures fit into the categories above and if you can make any new categories. Then choose the picture you like best and write down what you think the artist is trying to say in it.

A SUMMARY

Advent is the time when Christians get themselves ready for Christmas. It is a time to think seriously about the meaning of Jesus' coming. They think about his birth two thousand years ago and also about his promise to return.

Light and darkness are important symbols at Advent. Light stands for the Christian belief that Jesus came to show people the way to be really happy; he came to light their path. Darkness stands for the idea that some people would rather keep their evil ways hidden from God. Christians believe that when Jesus comes again he will judge these wicked people.

Light is also an important symbol of Christmas itself. Christmas is the joyful time when the church celebrates the birth of Jesus. The Christmas story also reminds Christians that it is a time for caring for others.

Many people find it easier to put across these religious ideas in pictures rather than in words. If you look at different paintings or statues of Mary with baby Jesus, you will see that the artists have expressed all sorts of ideas about them. Some make them very holy; others make them very human. Some show Jesus as a real baby whereas others cannot think of him as a helpless baby because they believe he is the all-powerful God.

- Orthodox Christians often have icons depicting the Nativity. In these sacred pictures Jesus is usually portrayed as a wise little man rather than a real baby. This is to show their belief that from the very beginning he was really the all-knowing God.

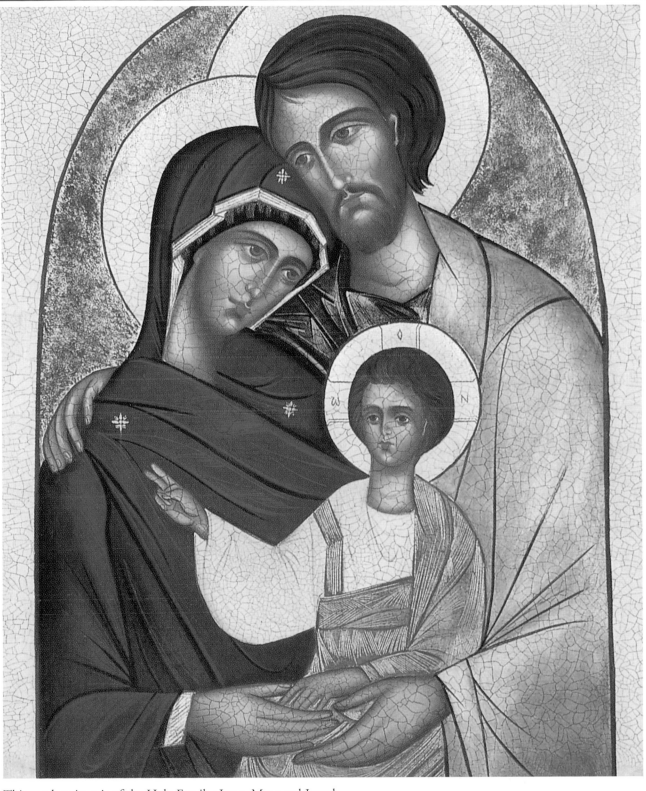

This modern icon is of the Holy Family: Jesus, Mary and Joseph

EPIPHANY

EPIPHANY

The feast of Epiphany is on 6 January, which begins the four weeks of Epiphany in the church's year. Epiphany sounds a very strange word in English. This is because it comes from a Greek word which means *'to make to appear, to reveal, to display'*. So at Epiphany Christians celebrate their belief that *Jesus was shown to the world as the Christ, the Saviour sent by God.*

At the church service the story of the Wise Men is read because it expresses this idea. It tells how wise men were led by God from distant lands to find the child Jesus and to realise his importance. It shows that although Jesus was born a Jew, he was sent by God for everyone, near and far.

Most of us know this story from Nativity plays and Christmas cards. Wise men from eastern countries were guided by an unusual star to Bethlehem where Jesus was born. When they found Jesus they worshipped him and gave him presents. Then they returned home, avoiding the king of the Jews, Herod the Great, who wanted information so that he could destroy the young Jesus before he became a threat to him. This story is only told in Saint Matthew's Gospel. You will find it in Matthew chapter 2. You can read the story for yourself and answer all the following questions, or go straight from question 1 to question 8.

ASSIGNMENTS

1 Write down the meaning of Epiphany. You can either explain it in your own words, or use the words in italics to make a sentence.

2 Where did the wise men go first of all in their search for 'the king of the Jews'?

3 What made Herod think that the child would be born in Bethlehem?

4 How did God warn the wise men to return home another way?

5 How was Joseph warned to flee from Herod?

6 What can we learn about Herod from the whole of this chapter?

7 Is it possible for a star to point directly to a particular house?

8 Illustrate one scene from this story or find a picture of it from an old Christmas card which you can stick into your book and label.

9 Look up a hymn book or carol sheet and copy out a carol about the wise men.

If you know the story of the wise men you probably talk of the Three Kings and you may even know that traditionally they are called Melchior, Caspar and Balthazar. We learn many of these details from carols like:

'Three kings from Persian lands afar
To Jordan follow the pointing star...'

This just shows how much a story grows over the years. Matthew's Gospel does not tell us how many men were involved, nor their names, nor that they were kings. But these are only small details, added to make the story more colourful; they do not change the original meaning of the story, celebrated at Epiphany.

SYMBOLIC OBJECTS

We have not yet mentioned what sort of gifts the wise men brought for the Christ: gold, frankincense and myrrh. They were not just expensive and exotic presents but each had a meaning, each was symbolic and said something important about Jesus.

- Gold was money. By offering this to Jesus the wise men were giving riches fit for a king, representing his wealth and power.

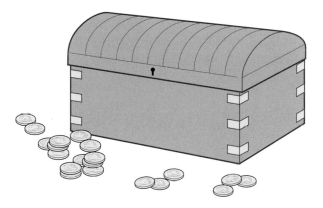

- Frankincense was a substance which was burnt in the worship of God; it gave off a cloud of sweet-smelling fragrance. Incense is still burnt at many

church services today (you may know what joss-sticks smell like, which are similar). By offering frankincense to Jesus the wise men were showing that they worshipped him as God.

- Myrrh was an ointment used to embalm dead bodies.

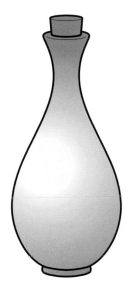

By offering myrrh to Jesus the wise men were symbolising the fact that Jesus must suffer and die.

We are still used to this idea of symbolic gifts today. On your birthday you may have a cake with the right number of candles on it to represent your age. Some cakes are made in special shapes: they may look like guitars, or chessboards or trains. These are given to people who have a special interest in such things. Love may be expressed in gifts like a red rose, a heart-shaped locket or a Valentine card. When couples become engaged the man usually buys his fiancée a ring with a beautiful stone in it, perhaps a diamond. There is a saying 'Diamonds are forever' and the engagement ring is a symbol of their promise to get married and stay with one another always.

ASSIGNMENTS

10 Draw the three gifts of the wise men and label them with their symbolic meanings.

11 What are the traditional gifts for confirmation, a silver wedding and retirement?

12 What other symbolic gifts can you think of?

When you begin to think about it you will find that there are many objects which are used for their symbolic value, just like the gold, frankincense and myrrh in this story. Many of these things are religious objects. The Bible, for instance, is sometimes used as a symbol. In court the witness is made to swear an oath on the Bible because it is a symbol of everything that is both sacred and true.

At weddings

If you have ever attended a church wedding you will perhaps remember some of the symbolic objects which are used on such an occasion. You will see that some of these symbols have deep religious meanings, whereas others are little more than superstition.

The most important symbol connected with a wedding is the ring. A ring is circular, the perfect shape because it has no beginning and no end. This symbolises the unending love between the marriage partners. The wedding ring is worn on the third finger of the left hand. This is because it was always believed that the vein from this finger ran straight to the heart, which is another symbol of love. You will spot the wedding cars by the white ribbons tied on them as a sign of celebration. The special clothes the guests wear, like the best hats and button-holes, are also signs that it is an important and happy occasion. Traditionally the bride dresses in pure white and has a veil which symbolises modesty. After the service people throw confetti. It does not achieve anything in itself but, apart from the fun of it, it

(a) How do you know that this is a church wedding?

(b) From the expressions on their faces, describe how you think they are feeling at this moment.

(c) Describe the costume of the groom. Why is he wearing these special clothes?

(d) Describe the bride's clothes thinking especially about the colour and her head-gear.

is a pretty, modern substitute for rice or seeds. These stood for fertility, growth and new life. Also, people give the bride and groom symbols to hold like cardboard black-cats, sweeps and horseshoes, or plastic handcuffs, or tin-openers. Then later the guests give the newly-weds presents, usually to help them set up home together and to wish them well.

So far we have been thinking especially of symbolic objects but we cannot leave the wedding scene without also thinking of some of the important symbolic actions which take place there. The bride arrives at the church with her father who leads her down the aisle and during the service 'gives her away' to the groom. He does this symbolically by taking her hand and passing it over to be held by the groom. This is supposed to show that the bride no longer belongs to her father, but to her husband, although today it is more fair to say that the bride and groom belong to each other. Then the priest binds together the hands of the bride and groom with the scarf that hangs round his neck. This symbolises that they are now joined together in marriage. At this stage, if the bride's face has been covered by a veil, she will throw back the veil to let her husband kiss her. This shows that from now on there will be no barriers between them. The music, the smiles, the congratulations and the ringing bells at the end of the service as the couple emerge hand in hand are all signs of the happiness of all concerned. When the wedding is over it is a tradition that the bride throws her bouquet towards her guests and whoever catches it is supposed to be the next to get married.

ASSIGNMENTS

13 List all the things that the bride may be given to hold immediately after the service, like a cardboard horseshoe. Say what each object stands for.

14 Think about the explanation given above and then explain what you are really wishing on the bride and groom when you throw confetti over them.

JESUS' BAPTISM

The other biblical story which is read at Epiphany is that of the baptism of Jesus because here again Jesus is shown to the people as the Son of God. The first three gospels, Matthew, Mark and Luke, all record how Jesus went down to the River Jordan where the prophet John the Baptist was publicly baptising many people. Matthew's Gospel tells the story in this way:

> 'Then Jesus arrived at the Jordan from Galilee, and came to John to be baptized by him. John tried to dissuade him. "Do you come to me?" he said; "I need rather to be baptized by you." Jesus replied, "Let it be so for the present; we do well to conform in this way with all that God requires." John then allowed him to come. After baptism Jesus came up out of the water at once, and at that moment heaven opened; he saw the Spirit of God descending like a dove to alight upon him; and a voice from heaven was heard saying, "This is my Son, my Beloved, on whom my favour rests." (Matthew 3:13-17)

What do you think really happened at Jesus' baptism? Was the sky really torn open? If video cameras had existed in first-century Palestine, could the onlookers have photographed God's Spirit coming down on Jesus like a bird? If they had had a cassette recorder with them, could they have recorded the voice of God and played it back later?

Of course we shall never know for sure, but it could be that the writer was using picture language to put across the real meaning of the incident as he understood it. Perhaps we are to understand things in this story as symbols. Just consider how we still use symbolic, picture language today. We might say of the weather 'It's raining cats and dogs' or 'All of a sudden the heavens opened and it poured with rain.' What do you think the writer meant when he said 'heaven opened'? Could there have been a sudden storm with forked lightning looking as though it

were splitting up the sky? Or perhaps the clouds parted to let through the sun? Or whatever happened, is the writer more concerned to emphasise that the message Jesus received was really from God? So he said that the voice came from heaven, which ancient people believed was God's dwelling place up above the sky.

What about the Spirit 'descending like a dove'? Are we meant to understand that God the Holy Spirit really *looks* like a bird, or even like a white ghostly shape? Could it mean that the Spirit is 'like a dove' in some other way? Just think how we still say things like 'You ass', or sometimes children are called 'kids' which are really baby goats, and some people call their babies 'my lamb' or 'you little monkey'. This is because *in some way* people are like these animals. We might say, for instance, that someone is as quiet as a mouse or as stubborn as a mule. Perhaps in this story, by using the symbol of the dove, the writer is saying that God came to Jesus quietly and gently, silently growing in him. People still ask God to come into their lives, but they do not expect to *see* him come in!

Lastly, we are told that a voice from heaven *was heard*. If you imagine that there was a storm breaking at the time, then perhaps it was thunder that the people heard, or the wind. Or again, perhaps we are not meant to take this literally, that is, to think that there was an actual voice which could have been recorded. If we understand it symbolically we are saying that this is trying to express a religious idea which would

be very difficult to explain in the normal way. Don't people still say 'God spoke to me' when they mean that they felt compelled in some strange way to do something, and thought that this was God guiding them? We talk about the voice of our conscience, and you may have been told to listen to your conscience when you are tempted to do wrong. But we do not expect actually to hear it with our ears. This is a symbolic way of talking. Perhaps the writer is using this symbol of hearing a voice to show that it was at his baptism that Jesus really became convinced of his special relationship with God the Father.

ASSIGNMENTS

15 We shall never know for sure what happened at Jesus' baptism, but we can all have our own opinions. Try to draw a picture of what you think you would have *seen* if you had been there. If you think that a lot of the story is symbolic then you would only have seen John dipping Jesus under the water, or maybe splashing the water over his head. Or you may think that the heavens and the dove and the voice were all literally true, in which case you must draw them.

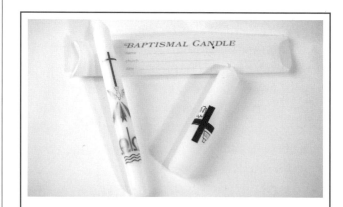

In some churches, candles are given for babies at their baptism.

(a) *What do the symbols on these candles stand for?*

(b) *Design your own symbol(s) for a baptism candle.*

(c) *Ask your teacher to make a collection of baptism candles for school.*

It is a tradition for Christian pilgrims to the Holy Land to be baptised in the River Jordan. Even if they have already been baptised, they can still be dipped in the water in a service to renew their baptism promises.

(a) How do you think these Christians feel being baptised in the same river as Jesus was baptised in?

A SUMMARY

Epiphany is the period of the church's year immediately after Christmas. It begins with the festival of Epiphany on 6 January and lasts for four weeks. It is a time of celebration and thanksgiving for the belief that Jesus was made known to all the world.

The story of the Wise Men is told. It shows Christians that Jesus was meant to be the Saviour of everyone, not just the Jews. Therefore people came from distant lands to see him. The story of Jesus' baptism, when he was grown up, also brings out this idea that Jesus was publicly shown to be God.

There are symbols in both these stories. The gifts of the wise men were symbolic just as gifts like wedding rings are still symbolic today. Gold stood for Jesus' kingship; frankincense showed that he was believed to be God; and myrrh represented his death.

There are also many parts of the baptism story which could be symbolic. We are told that heaven opened, the Spirit came down on Jesus like a dove, and that the voice of God spoke to him. This could be picture language, or symbols, to show that on this occasion God really did get in touch with Jesus in a very special way which is difficult to describe in normal words.

Some pilgrims to the Holy Land take a bottle of River Jordan water home with them. *Try to find out what they might do with it.*

Jordan River Water Holy-Land

LENT

LENT

The word 'Lent' simply refers to the time of year when the days lengthen: in other words, spring. It comes from the Latin word *lentum*. Most of us know when Lent is about to start because of Pancake Day. Many towns still organise a traditional pancake race, and most children badger their mothers into frying them endless pancakes which are liberally coated with sugar. The best part is tossing the pancake in the air and watching anxiously to see whether it is going to stick to the ceiling or land safely back in the greased pan.

ASSIGNMENTS

1 As a class, discuss what special events you have been involved in on Pancake Day.

2 What are pancakes made from?

3 Explain why pancakes are suitable for Shrove Tuesday.

All this fun and food was necessary when the majority of people in Christian countries took Lent seriously. It was kept as a long, strict religious fast when people gave up all rich food. The day before Lent starts is properly called Shrove Tuesday because people went to church to be 'shriven'. This means they confessed their sins to the priest and were forgiven. Then they collected together all the foods which they had to go without during Lent and used them up. This included eggs and butter and that is why pancakes became the traditional food on this day. In France this day is called 'Mardi Gras' which means 'Fat Tuesday'.

Lent itself begins with Ash Wednesday and lasts for six and a half weeks. It ends at Easter when Christians remember the execution of Jesus and then celebrate his rising from death. This length of time allows for forty fast days and Sundays. Christians have always fasted before Easter to some degree, both to prepare themselves for this, the greatest of Christian festivals, and also because Jesus is said to have fasted in the desert for forty days. Luke's Gospel says:

'Full of the Holy Spirit, Jesus returned from the Jordan, and for forty days was led by the Spirit up and down the wilderness and tempted by the devil. All that time he had nothing to eat, and at the end of it he was famished.' (Luke 4:1-2)

The New Testament shows this as a time of testing for Jesus, before he began his life's work to which God had called him. It was probably necessary for him to be alone in prayer to test his strength for the work of preaching and healing that lay ahead of him.

Lent is still a difficult period for those Christians who keep it today. The church no longer imposes a strict fast but it is a time when some Christians try to overcome their own faults because they believe that it was human sin which led Jesus to be crucified. They try to follow the example of Jesus in the wilderness by giving up luxuries and practising self-discipline. And they try to put aside more time for prayer and religious acts so that they can really let God guide their lives.

ASSIGNMENTS

4 Read the story of Jesus' Temptations in full in Luke 4:1-13.

5 Are there any times in the day or night when you are completely alone? How do you feel about being alone? Can you imagine a particular situation when you would want to be alone?

6 What sort of tests do you have at school or elsewhere? Can you see any purpose in being tested?

7 Have you ever given up something for a person or for a cause? Why did you do it? How did it make you feel? Would you do it again?

8 Why can it be useful sometimes to 'go without'?

9 What kind of things do people give up during Lent?

10 What extra things could Christians do during Lent to help them understand God better and the plan he has for their lives?

SYMBOLS OF SORROW

We have seen that Lent is a serious time for Christians. So the church traditionally uses purple as its symbolic colour; it takes away any bright decorations like flowers; and it covers up any crosses, pictures or statues with sackcloth. Also, on Ash Wednesday some Christians will smear a cross of ash on their foreheads. The

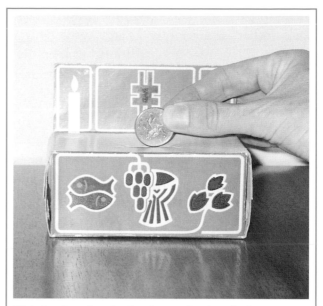

This is a Lent box in the shape of a church altar.
(a) What do you think it is for?
(b) Whom could you ask about it?

ashes come from burnt up palm crosses kept from Palm Sunday of the previous year. So both the church buildings and Christians themselves are dressed for this solemn occasion.

This is not as strange as it may sound because most of us wear different clothes for different occasions and decorate our homes in suitable ways. If we were attending a sad, sombre event like a funeral we would probably wear dark colours. People often wear black at funerals, even if it is just a black armband. Some people dress completely in black, with the women wearing

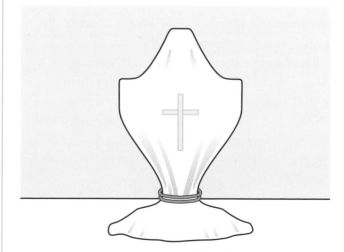

This shows a cross covered in sackcloth.

black veils; and Travellers continue to wear smart black clothes for several weeks afterwards. This affects buildings too. It is traditional to keep the curtains closed until after the funeral in a house where someone has died, particularly if the corpse is laid out there.

All the things the church does during Lent are for the same reason. Sackcloth and ashes no longer mean much to us but in the Bible they are symbols of sorrow and mourning. At Chinese funerals even today the widows dress in sackcloth robes and the other mourners wear sashes of coarse sackcloth around their waists. Another sign of sorrow recorded in the Bible is the tearing of your clothes.

ASSIGNMENTS

11 Look up the following biblical passages and copy out the references to sackcloth and ashes: Psalm 35:13; 2 Samuel 3:31; Luke 10:13.

12 Why do people often look dishevelled when they are very upset?

13 What else do people do when they are very sad? (Think about what you do when you are unhappy.)

PALM SUNDAY

Palm Sunday is the title given by the church to the Sunday before Easter. It is the beginning of what has come to be known as Holy Week, the last week of Lent. Since the fourth century this week has been observed by the church to remember the events immediately leading up to Jesus' death. During this week pious Christians attend many services to help themselves to understand as fully as possible the meaning of the death and resurrection of Jesus Christ.

Palm Sunday is a joyful occasion when Christians remember Jesus' triumphant entry into the holy city of Jerusalem. Mark's Gospel says:

> 'So they brought the colt to Jesus and spread their cloaks on it, and he mounted. And people carpeted the road with their cloaks, while others spread brushwood which they had cut in the fields; and those who went ahead and the others who came behind shouted, "Hosanna! Blessings on him who comes in the name of the Lord! Blessings on the coming kingdom of our father David! Hosanna in the heavens!"' (Mark 11:7-10)

On this occasion Jesus was publicly proclaimed as the Saviour or Messiah for whom the Jews had been waiting. 'Hosanna' meant 'save (us) now'; his followers believed he had been sent by God to save his people, following in the footsteps of their great king David of old. The people waved palm branches, which is a Jewish festival custom, and they spread their coats on the ground in his way, to show how important he was. In the same way Sir Walter Raleigh is said to have spread his cloak across a puddle for Queen Elizabeth I to walk on.

ASSIGNMENTS

14 What does it mean if someone says they will 'put out the red carpet' for you? Where does this idea come from?

15 What things do people wave today at festivals and other joyful public occasions? (For example, at football matches, at the last night of the Proms and when watching royal processions.)

An open-air Palm Sunday procession in Spain.

(a) What are the people waving, and why?

On Palm Sunday the church tries to recreate the festival spirit of Jesus' triumphal entry into Jerusalem. Church buildings are usually decorated with palm branches and there are big processions, often with the whole congregation joining in. In hot countries the procession may go outside the church building and sometimes a real donkey is used. It is also a custom to make small crosses from dried palm leaves. During the service these are blessed by the priest and then everyone is given a cross to keep. This reminds the worshippers that, although Palm Sunday is a happy time, it was not long before the joyful 'Hosannas' turned to shouts of 'Crucify him' and within the week they will be remembering Jesus' death on a cross.

Ride on! ride on in majesty!
Hark, all the tribes hosanna cry;
Thine humble beast pursues his road
With palms and scattered garments strowed.

Ride on! ride on in majesty!
The winged squadrons of the sky
Look down with sad and wondering eyes
To see the approaching sacrifice.

Ride on! ride on in majesty!
In lowly pomp ride on to die;
Bow thy meek head to mortal pain,
Then take, O God, thy power, and reign.

A SUMMARY

Lent is the period of the church's year before Easter. It lasts for forty days because Jesus is said to have spent forty days alone in the desert. Whilst there he prayed and went without food and this is what Christians do at Lent, to different degrees. The day before Lent is known as Pancake Day. Years ago the church insisted that people kept a strict fast during Lent, and so they used up all their eggs and butter in pancakes the day before. During Lent the church buildings are usually very dull and the colour purple is used. This shows that it is a serious time for Christians.

The last week of Lent is known as Holy Week and begins on Palm Sunday. This is a day of light relief because Christians celebrate Jesus' entry into Jerusalem when he was proclaimed as king and people waved palm branches in their joy. On this day crosses, made from dried palm leaves, are given out at the church service. This reminds Christians that they must now think very seriously about the death of Jesus.

JESUS' DEATH

MAUNDY THURSDAY

The Thursday before Easter is known as Maundy Thursday. This comes from the Latin word *mandatum* which means a 'mandate' or 'command'. It refers to the new commandment which Jesus gave his disciples. John's Gospel tells us that this happened at the last meeting Jesus had with his disciples before his death, now called the Last Supper. During the meal Jesus got up and, tying a towel around him, he began to wash the feet of his disciples. Then he explained that he had done this to set them an example and said:

> ' "I give you a new commandment: love one another; as I have loved you, so you are to love one another. If there is love among you, then all will know that you are my disciples." '
> (John 13:34-35)

If you lived in a hot country like Palestine you would wear sandals and your feet would get very hot and dusty. It was the custom in Jesus' day for the servants to wash the feet of guests, just as today we may expect to be helped off with our coat and relieved of a dripping umbrella. So what Jesus did was not really as strange as it sounds, except that it was the wrong way round. We would have expected Jesus' disciples to act as the servants, not Jesus himself. By this action Jesus was driving home the fact that love is not just a matter of words or even of feelings but it is what you do. Christians learn from this story that they should humbly serve one another if they want to follow in Christ's footsteps.

As with many incidents in Jesus' life, this is sometimes acted out in church services. In some churches the clergy wash the feet of a few members of the congregation on Maundy Thursday. I expect those chosen wash their feet thoroughly beforehand. This does not matter because it is done to remind people of what Jesus did and is therefore a symbol of Christian love and service. It used to be traditional for all important people – the monarch, lords, bishops, and abbots – to wash the feet of twelve poor men on this day to represent the twelve disciples. This has largely fallen out of use although the Pope still does it in Saint Peter's Cathedral in Rome, the centre of the Catholic Church.

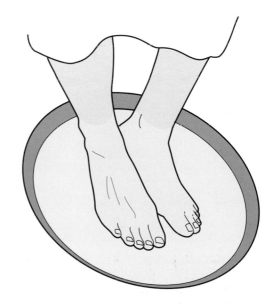

In England the Queen continues a six hundred-year-old custom when she gives out 'Maundy Money' to a selection of old age pensioners and the choir members. Each year on Maundy Thursday the royal service is held at a different cathedral and the money consists of specially minted silver pennies, one for each year of the Queen's life. The clergy at the service still wear a towel over their shoulders to symbolise the original practice of foot-washing.

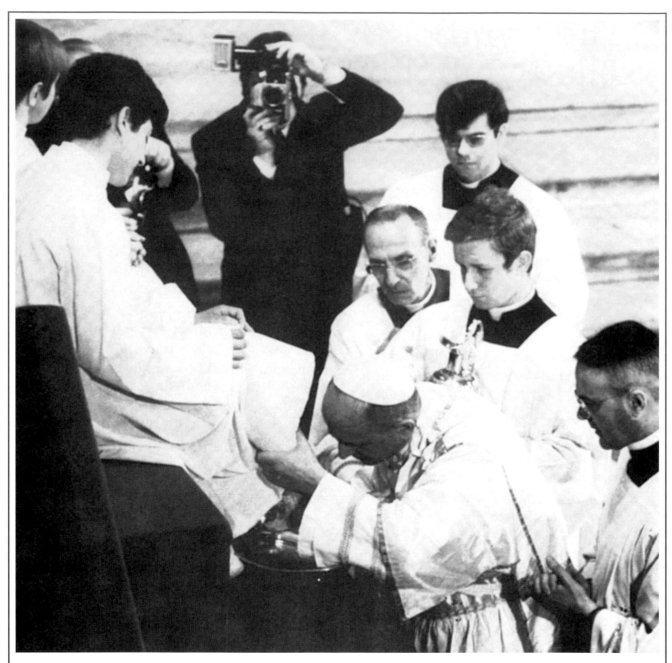

This photo shows Pope Paul VI. This is not the current pope.

(a) *What is he doing for the boy in the picture?*

(b) *Remembering that the Pope is acting out what Jesus did to his disciples, say how many boys should be involved in this ceremony.*

(c) *Why do you think the men in the background are so keen to photograph this?*

(d) *How do you think you would feel if you were the boy in this photograph?*

ASSIGNMENTS

1 What was the new commandment which Jesus gave his disciples?

2 How did Jesus demonstrate this command?

3 Some Christians call this new commandment 'the eleventh commandment' since there are already Ten Commandments in the Bible. Do you think this is meant to be just one more commandment, or could a person lead a good life by following this rule alone?

4 Discuss ways you could be of service to others.

The Last Supper took place on Thursday evening, before Jesus' death the next day. The gospels tell us that, after the meal, Jesus went with his disciples into the Garden of Gethsemane which is in a valley just outside Jerusalem. There he found strength in prayer to go through with the dreadful ordeal that awaited him. It was there that he was arrested and taken off for trial.

Many churches, therefore, hold a service on the evening of Maundy Thursday to remember all these events. At the end of the service it is traditional to strip bare the altar to symbolise the sordidness and bleakness of all that happened to Jesus that night. The story goes that Jesus' disciples fell asleep in the garden and that Jesus roused them with the words: 'Were you not able to stay awake for one hour? Stay awake, all of you; and pray that you may be spared the test. The spirit is willing, but the flesh is weak.' (Mark 14:38.) For this reason some churches keep a vigil for one hour after the service has ended. This means they stay awake and pray in the darkened church. Other churches organise an all-night vigil in which different members of the congregation take turns to stay for about an hour each.

THE SYMBOL OF BREAD AND WINE

It seems that at the Last Supper Jesus was aware that his death was near. So he took two things from the meal in order to leave two symbols of himself for the time when his followers would no longer be able to see and touch him. The earliest account we have of this event is in the first letter written by Saint Paul to the Christians at Corinth. There he said:

> '...the Lord Jesus, on the night of his arrest, took bread and, after giving thanks to God, broke it and said: "This is my body, which is for you; do this as a memorial of me." In the same way, he took the cup after supper, and said: "This cup is the new covenant sealed by my blood. Whenever you drink it, do this as a memorial of me." ' (I Corinthians 11:24-25)

The Old Testament tells how the Jews entered into a special agreement, or covenant, with God. Christians believe that, by dying, Jesus signed a new agreement so that from then on people could find their salvation by following him.

ASSIGNMENTS

5 Draw the two symbols that Jesus left for his disciples.
6 What does each symbol represent?

After Jesus' death his followers acted out what had happened at the Last Supper, in obedience to his command to do it in memory of him. Christians have continued to do this ever since in their most important services in which bread and wine are consecrated, that is, they are specially set apart, to represent Jesus himself. This symbolism can be seen in the names used for this bread – Catholics call it 'the host'; this comes from the Latin word *hostia* meaning 'victim' because they relive the sacrifice of Christ at every mass. The Orthodox call it 'the Lamb' since Jesus is called the Lamb of God in the New Testament and lambs were used for sacrifice.

The Orthodox priest takes a small knife and pierces the side of the loaf just as Jesus' side is said to have been pierced by a sword when he was hanging dead on the cross. In all churches the bread is broken so that it can be shared out amongst those taking part, called the communicants. This represents the fact that Jesus' body was broken, or killed, on the cross. The wine is poured out from a jug into the cup or cups from which the communicants will drink. Again this is symbolic because the poured wine represents Jesus' blood which was shed. Before his death only those who lived with Jesus could know him, but Christians believe that his death has now made him available to everyone who wants to know him - just as the bread and wine are shared out amongst all who come to take it.

Another word used for these symbols of bread and wine is 'sacrament'. Sacraments are the most important Christian symbols. Christians believe that God acts through them to help them live their lives in God's way.

The old-established Churches have seven sacraments:

1 bread and wine

2 baptism

3 confirmation

4 penance (also called reconciliation)

5 anointing with oil

6 ordination

7 marriage

These signs are all found in the New Testament. Protestants only call the first two of these 'sacraments' because these are the only two which Jesus himself commanded his followers to continue.

The service which includes this sacrament of bread and wine is known by several names.

- Catholics call it the Mass. This simply comes from the Latin word on which the service used to end when it spoke of 'sending' the worshippers back into their everyday world.

- More significant is the name Eucharist. This comes from a Greek word meaning 'thanksgiving'. It shows that it is a service when Christians thank God for his great love in sending them Jesus Christ.

- Another name for the service is Holy Communion. Communion means being at one with, or in union with, someone else. Christians say that they all belong together because of their religion. This service highlights this belief because they all share together in the bread and wine, just as if they were coming together for a friendly but special meal.

- It is also called The Lord's Supper or The Lord's Table by some Free Churches who want to show that the Last Supper is being remembered.

ASSIGNMENTS

7 List all the names given to this service and explain what they mean.

8 Think about the meals which you eat together with your family and friends. Consider whether the food or the company is more important and whether you would feel the same if you were eating alone.

9 Bread and wine are important symbolic foods for Christians. Can you think of any other foods which are symbolic (eg. what cakes are made for special occasions?).

There are different practices connected with this service in different churches. Orthodox Christians queue up and the priest gives them the bread and wine together from a spoon. Catholics stand before the altar where the laity are given the bread and if they wish, the wine. Anglicans kneel before the altar to receive the sacrament in both kinds: bread and wine. They all sip the wine in turn from one large cup, called a chalice, which emphasises the importance of sharing together.

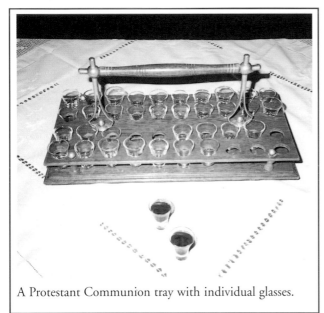

A Protestant Communion tray with individual glasses.

The Free Churches generally remain seated whilst glasses of grape juice and the bread are distributed to each of them, so that they can then all eat and drink together.

These different practices are not so important as the various ways in which the denominations understand this sacrament. For Orthodox and Catholic Christians the bread and wine do not just stand for, or remind them of, Christ's body and blood; the symbols are so powerful for them that they believe Jesus Christ is really present in them. Protestants however have always thought that too much emphasis on the sacraments could lead people to believe that they are Christians simply because they take the sacraments and not because of the experiences which they represent: experiences of Christ's forgiveness and of having a new start in life. In fact the Quakers and the Salvation Army feel so strongly about this that they do not use sacraments at all.

ASSIGNMENTS

10 Why do you think Jesus left real things for his followers to remember him by?

11 What sorts of things do you keep to help you remember your friends and relatives, particularly if they are far away or even dead? Or what souvenirs do you keep of places or events?

12 What dangers are there in becoming too attached to objects of sentimental value?

THE SYMBOL OF THE CROSS

The day after Maundy Thursday is called by Christians Good Friday. This seems a strange title for the saddest day in the church's year, the day when Christians remember the death of Jesus on a cross, and It may have begun as 'God's Friday'. Yet Christians believe that there is a sense in which Jesus' death was good because they see it as essential to God's plan to save mankind. Jesus' death is seen as a sacrifice. Christians say that Jesus offered up his own life in order to pay for the sins of all the world. They believe that people no longer have to make up for everything they have done wrong, nor do they have to earn a reward from God. Instead, they believe that Jesus freely offers them salvation.

Here is a collection of crosses: some are to be worn, some to be hung on the wall or stood on a shelf. Some are plain, some are ornate.

(a) As a class, make your own collection of crosses. Discuss the meaning of each cross, and why they are different.

It is difficult for us to really understand this idea of sacrifice but it was a common idea for the people in Jesus' day. The Jews then were used to offering sacrifices to God to pay for their sins; not human sacrifices but agricultural produce, such as Christians take to church at Harvest Festivals, as well as birds and animals.

ASSIGNMENTS

13 What sacrifices do most parents make for their children?

14 Would it be a sacrifice if you gave up something which you did not really want?

15 What do you think Christians mean when they talk about being 'a living sacrifice' for God?

Good Friday

Most Christians go to church on Good Friday and the services obviously have a heavy atmosphere because they are mourning the death of their Lord. Many churches have a continual three-hour service from midday until three o'clock in the afternoon, which is thought to be the time that Jesus hung dying on the cross. At some services a crucifix is held up for the people to come and kiss. This ceremony is called the veneration of the cross. They are not worshipping the cross itself but using it as a symbol of Christ and his death.

The cross is the central symbol of Christianity. On Good Friday you probably eat the traditional hot cross buns but you will also see crosses on church buildings, on Christian books like the Bible, and worn by people, usually around their necks. Also many Christians make the sign of the cross over their own bodies, touching first their forehead, then their chest and then their two shoulders. Orthodox Christians say that this represents the offering of their mind, heart and strength to God, and they repeat this action many, many times. Other Christians may not do it themselves but it is common for the priest to make the sign of the cross over the people as he gives the blessing in the name of God the Father, Son and Holy Spirit.

Down through the centuries this symbol of the cross has developed into a variety of shapes.

(i) The plain Latin cross is the most common symbol of Jesus' death.

(ii) The Saint Anthony's cross in the shape of the letter 'T' is probably a more realistic shape for the crosses which the Romans used for execution.

(iii) The Russian Orthodox cross shows the 'title' which was nailed to the top of the cross to publicise Jesus' crime, and also the bar to which his feet were secured.

(iv) The Greek cross became the emblem of Saint George.

(v) Other crosses became much more ornate and sometimes incorporated further symbols. For instance the Saint Andrew's cross is in the shape of the Greek letter which begins the word 'Christ'.

(vi) The Maltese cross has eight points which represent the eight blessings of Jesus recorded in the famous Sermon on the Mount. Today it is the badge of the Saint John Ambulance Brigade.

(vii) The Celtic cross includes a circle which represents eternity since a circle has no end and no beginning. The same is said of Christ.

(viii) Some crosses are set at the top of three steps which are said to represent faith, hope and love, the three main Christian virtues.

(ix) A crucifix is a cross which depicts the figure of Christ hanging on it.

(x) Sometimes the crucifix shows Christ the King instead of a dying man. This symbolises the Christian belief that the crucifixion was not a defeat for Jesus but really his triumph when he proved that he was the Saviour of the world.

ASSIGNMENTS

16 Draw and colour in the Union Jack which is a combination of three crosses. It has the red cross on white background of Saint George, the patron saint of England; the white X-shaped cross on a blue background of Saint Andrew, the patron saint of Scotland; and the thin red X-shaped cross of Saint Patrick, the patron saint of Ireland.

(a) In what sort of place was this photograph taken?

(b) How do you know that the cross in the foreground is foreign?

(c) Look at the list of crosses and find out from which country the dead person probably came.

(d) Why does this particular shape have three cross-bars on it?

This is a Passion Flower and is mostly found in South America. It is so called because 'passion' can mean suffering and many of the symbols of Jesus' crucifixion can be seen in it. Working outwards from the centre we can see the sign of the three nails with which Jesus was fixed to the cross; then the sign for the five wounds which were inflicted in his hands, feet, and side; then a part which looks like the crown of thorns which was forced onto Jesus' head; then the ten petals which stand for ten of the disciples, not including Judas Iscariot who betrayed Jesus, nor Peter who denied that he knew Jesus; lastly the twisting tendrils, with which the plant climbs, represent the hands and whips of his tormentors.

A SUMMARY

The Thursday of Holy Week is known as Maundy Thursday. On this day Christians remember the events of the Thursday before Jesus died, when he ate the Last Supper with his followers. At this meal he washed his disciples' feet as a sign that they should never be too proud to serve others. He gave them a new command, or *mandate*, to love one another. This is where our word 'Maundy' comes from.

The gospels tells us that at the Last Supper Jesus gave his disciples some bread to eat with the words 'This is my body'. Then he did the same with some wine, saying 'This is my blood'. Since then Christians have used bread and wine as a sacrament, or symbol, of Christ. They hold special services regularly when they act out what happened at the Last Supper and remember Jesus' death. This service is called by various names such as the Mass, Eucharist or Holy Communion.

Good Friday follows Maundy Thursday. It is the day set aside by Christians to remember Jesus' death on a cross. It is called 'good' because they believe that his death has made it possible for them to come to God. The cross is therefore a very important symbol of Christianity and has developed in many ways.

EASTER

BAPTISM

Holy Saturday is the last day of Holy Week and many churches hold services on this eve of Easter Day. In the early church this was always the time to baptise or 'christen' new Christian converts who had been learning about Christianity during Lent. They were then ready to take their first communion on Easter Sunday, the Day of Resurrection.

It was very fitting to have this sacrament then because Christian baptism symbolises death and resurrection. When people go down under the water it is a sign that they are being buried with all their selfish concerns; when they rise up out of the water, it is a sign that they are starting a new life with Christ to help them. It seems that this was what early Christian baptism was all about. Some of the early Christian fonts were even built to look like tombs so that the candidates could say, like Saint Paul:

> 'By baptism we were buried with him, and lay dead, in order that, as Christ was raised from the dead in the splendour of the Father, so also we might set our feet upon the new path of life.' (Romans 6:4)

Some Christian denominations try to keep to the New Testament idea of baptism which says that people being brought to Christianity for the first time were told to 'Believe and be baptised' and they usually went down into the water to do this. You can tell from its name that the Baptist church is the most insistent upon this. For them, baptism is for believers, in other words, people who are old enough to put their faith in Christ. The Baptists will make sure that they have access to a small pool of water into which the minister and the candidate will wade so that the new Christian can be ducked right under the water. The candidate may wear white clothes which can easily be changed afterwards, but the minister may dress up in waders which come up to his thighs so that he can continue the service. These baptisms are very moving occasions especially as the new Christian will usually make a public testimony beforehand, explaining how he or she came to believe in Jesus Christ.

ASSIGNMENTS

1 What is meant by believer's baptism?

2 Draw two pictures of a baptism, showing a person ducked under the water, and then standing up in the water afterwards. Underneath, say what these two actions mean.

Total immersion in water is certainly a very dramatic symbol but most Christians would say that it is not necessary. As with all symbols, it is the meaning that counts and the same meaning is seen in simply splashing water over the head of the candidate. Baptism is also understood to be a sign of inner cleansing. We all use water to wash with, and so the baptismal washing can stand for the belief that God is washing away a person's sins.

These ideas connected with baptism are a little hard to understand when we realise that most Christians practise infant baptism rather than believer's baptism. In the Orthodox church the baby, while still very small, is undressed and immersed three times in a large tub of water. In other churches the fonts often hold only a small amount of water. This is blessed by the priest and splashed three times over the baby's head and then the sign of the cross is made on its forehead.

(a) Notice that this pool has been built specially for the purpose and therefore where do you think this baptism is taking place?

(b) How do you think you would feel if this were you?

(c) Try to find someone who has been baptised in this way. Ask them why it was important for them.

(d) Is there anything for which you would 'stand up and be counted'?

Some of you may be wondering how a little baby can have any sins to be washed away or how it can be called a Christian. Yet many Christians do believe that babies need to be cleansed by God. They believe in 'original sin'; in other words, they say that every human being is basically selfish and needs to be taught by God to put other people first. This does not come naturally. Infant baptism is seen as setting the child's feet on the road to becoming an active Christian. It is a recognition of the tremendous influence parents have over their children so that, if the parents are practising Christians, there is every reason to expect that the children will learn about Christianity and join in church activities. Usually the parents invite a few relatives or friends to become Godparents to their baby at the baptism. Together they promise to help the child to grow up as a true Christian. They may be given a card like this one.

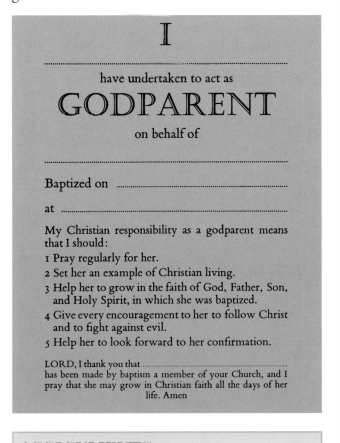

I

....

have undertaken to act as

GODPARENT

on behalf of

....

Baptized on ....

at ....

My Christian responsibility as a godparent means that I should:

1 Pray regularly for her.

2 Set her an example of Christian living.

3 Help her to grow in the faith of God, Father, Son, and Holy Spirit, in which she was baptized.

4 Give every encouragement to her to follow Christ and to fight against evil.

5 Help her to look forward to her confirmation.

LORD, I thank you that ....
has been made by baptism a member of your Church, and I pray that she may grow in Christian faith all the days of her life. Amen

ASSIGNMENTS

3 Discuss what you think is the best age for baptism.

CONFIRMATION

Since babies cannot speak for themselves at baptism, there is another service for when they are grown-up and can make their own consent to these promises. This is called confirmation which means being established more firmly as a Christian. It used to be the custom for Catholics to be confirmed at the age of about seven and it made a very pretty picture to see all the little girls dressed in white dresses and veils, as though they were brides of Christ. Most Catholic churches now prefer young people to be at least teenagers before they go through with this serious personal commitment. They can, however, receive communion beforehand, so that they are fully involved in the worship of the church.

The importance of believers' confirmation is shown by the fact that it is always conducted by a bishop. He places his hand on the candidate's head as he prays that the Spirit of God will increasingly work through him or her. Catholics are also anointed with oil at confirmation. This is a sign of inner healing since oil or greasy creams are rubbed into cuts and burns to help them to heal. Also at Catholic services the bishop lightly slaps the face of each candidate with two fingers. This is a sign of punishment for all the sins the Christian has committed since baptism. They are now put behind him or her with this fresh start in the Christian life. After Christians have been confirmed they are accepted as full adult members of the church and are allowed to take the sacrament representing the body and blood of Christ. This serves as a continual reminder of the central Christian belief in Christ's death and resurrection and most Christians find that it gives them strength to be responsible members of the church.

It is perhaps surprising to find that in the Orthodox church there is no further service of confirmation, but after baptism the baby is anointed with holy oil and is then given the bread and wine. Yet this reminds Christians that the sacraments are God's gift to men and women, through which he works; rather than stressing the importance of the Christian's response to God. It also emphasises the idea that the sacraments are mysteries which Christians will never fully understand, however old they are.

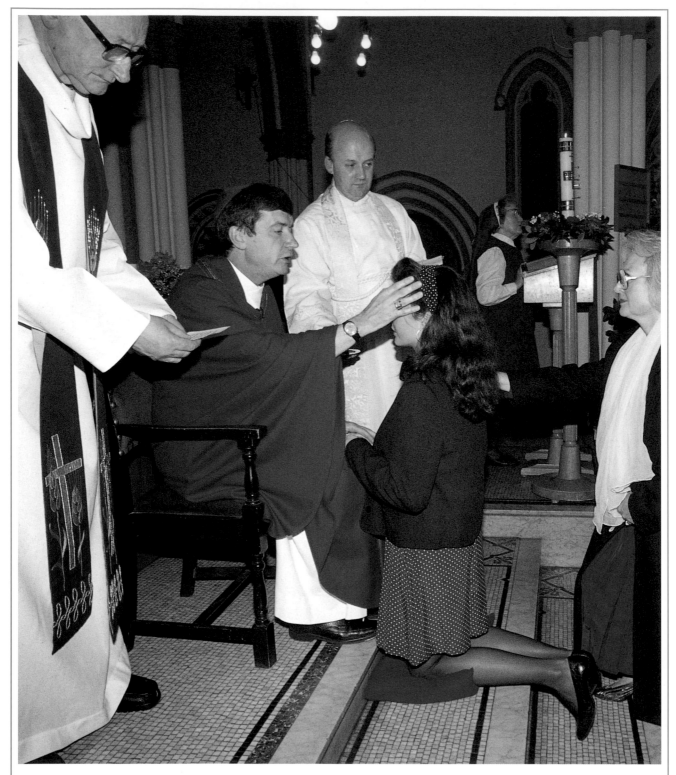

(a) Write your own caption to this photograph, as full as possible. Try to explain who the various people are, what is happening and why.

EASTER SUNDAY

Easter Day is the most joyful festival of the church; it is the feast of feasts. After the long weeks of Lent and the mounting sorrow of Holy Week, Easter Sunday brings a feeling of joy and excitement. The church buildings are brightly decorated and rousing hymns of praise are sung at the services. Christians proclaim that their Lord Jesus who was dead and buried has now risen from the grave and lives for evermore. All four gospels tell in great detail how his tomb was found empty on the Sunday morning and how, through various experiences, his followers became convinced that Jesus had conquered death and was really with them once more. This is the heart of the Christian message for, without belief in the Resurrection, there would be no belief in the importance of Jesus as the Christ, the Saviour, the Son of God.

ASSIGNMENTS

4 Music can often express feelings far better than words. Try to find some Easter music such as an Easter hymn. First copy out some of the words; then describe the mood that the music creates.

This excitement of Easter Day is perhaps felt most strongly in the Orthodox church because of the long and elaborate service in which the Easter ideas are expressed. Orthodox Christians arrive late on Saturday night for a service which will last about four hours. Inside the building is a flower-covered coffin at which they pay their respects just as if the dead body of Jesus were lying there. Each person holds a candle which lights the church and at midnight the building is vacated and the doors closed, leaving it in total darkness, to represent the closed tomb of Christ. Then the cry goes up from the priest 'Christ is risen', to which the people reply 'He is risen indeed'. The congregation re-enter the building for the rest of the service. The opening of the doors represents the rolling away of the stone from Jesus' tomb.

In Catholic and many Anglican churches a Paschal Candle is lit on Holy Saturday night. This is a huge candle which remains alight for all the services during the next forty days until Ascension Day. This shows that out of the darkness and despair of Christ's death came the light and hope of his Resurrection. During this period the candle stands for the belief that Christ, the 'Light of the World', still appeared on earth to his followers to convince them that he had really conquered death once and for all. Another sign of this is an empty cross, rather than a crucifix; this reminds Christians that Jesus did not end here.

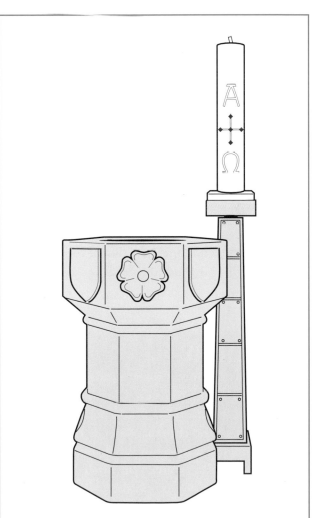

After the Easter season, the Paschal candle is stood by the font and the small baptism candles are lit from it. This is a symbol that Christians share in Jesus' new life.

(a) *Find out what the symbols on the Paschal candle represent.*

There are many other symbols of resurrection which Christians use at Eastertime. Many of these were symbols of new life even before Christianity began and were used to celebrate the coming of Spring; the word 'Easter' comes from *Eostre*, the name of the Anglo-Saxon goddess of dawn and spring. You will already know several of these symbols. For instance, lots of children have chocolate Easter eggs or decorate the shells of hard-boiled eggs. Eggs represent a life about to begin because the young chicks hatch out of them. Other animals like bunnies and lambs also remind us of new life. Then all around us at Eastertime we are aware of the greenery, the blossom on the trees and the fresh spring flowers like daffodils. Another symbol is the butterfly: a beautiful creature which emerges from a chrysalid. The church uses all of these symbols to represent the new life which they believe Christ was given at his resurrection and offers to all those who follow him.

ASSIGNMENTS

5 Draw as many symbols of resurrection as you can.

6 If Christians really believe that they will share in Jesus' resurrection-life, how should they feel about dying, or about the death of someone they love?

Not only is the Resurrection celebrated on Easter Sunday but on every Sunday of the year. Jesus and his first followers were Jews who kept Saturday as their holy day. After the Resurrection, Christians chose Sunday as the most important day of the week so this became the Christian holy day when most of the church services are held.

A SUMMARY

On the day before Easter Sunday it used to be traditional to baptise new Christians. This is the sacrament which shows that a person has become a member of the church. Water is the sign that is used. Sometimes a person is baptised by being put right under the water. In other churches the person's head alone is splashed with water. Some churches, like the Baptist church, say that people must be old enough to believe in Jesus Christ before being baptised. Other churches baptise babies and then have another service when the children are old enough to answer for themselves. This is called confirmation.

Easter Sunday itself is the most joyful time of the church's year. It celebrates the Christian belief that Jesus rose from the grave and lives for evermore.

On this day Christians decorate the church buildings with beautiful flowers, they dress up in their best clothes, and sing happy songs in the services. There are many things they use to symbolise the resurrection and new life, like eggs, bunnies and butterflies. Even the Christian holy day, which is Sunday, was chosen to remind them of the Resurrection.

TRINITY

ASCENSION

To ascend means to go up, and on Ascension Day Christians remember the story from the New Testament of how Jesus eventually left his disciples forty days after his resurrection. We are told: '...as they watched, he was lifted up, and a cloud removed him from their sight.' (The Acts of the Apostles 1:9b)

This is a very strange story if it is to be taken literally. It implies that heaven is somewhere 'up there', and that Jesus lives there in bodily form. Yet we would not expect to see Jesus through a telescope. And what do we say to people living on the other side of the world? Our 'up' is their 'down'. But of course, when this story was written, people still believed in a flat earth, covered by the dome of the sky with heaven above it. So to say that Jesus was lifted up in a cloud was to say that he was going to be with God.

We still use the symbolism of height today and this can help us to appreciate this story. We talk about being 'top of the form' or 'bottom of the class'; 'on top of the world' or 'down in the dumps'. We can speak of 'looking up to' someone in admiration or 'looking down on' someone we despise. None of this is to be taken literally; it is picture language. In the same way, on Ascension Day, Christians speak of Jesus being taken *up* into heaven and reigning on *high*. These are ways of expressing belief in his greatness. Christians believe that Christ is no longer tied to an earthly form but, as God, he rules the whole universe.

This is frequently found in the New Testament as in the following passage:

'Therefore God raised him to the heights and bestowed on him the name above all names, that at the name of Jesus every knee should bow - in heaven, on earth, and in the depths - and every tongue confess, "Jesus Christ is Lord", to the glory of God the Father.' (Philippians 2:9-11)

It helps Christians to think of Christ as being up above them because they can imagine him looking down on everyone and helping people wherever they are, whereas when he lived on earth he could only be with a few people at a time.

ASSIGNMENTS

1 Can you think of any other symbolic sayings about height or directions?

2 Look up a similar passage to the one above in Ephesians 1:20-21. Why is Jesus said to be at God's right hand?

3 Draw a picture to illustrate the idea of Christ in glory looking down on the world.

This is how an artist has shown the Ascension of Christ.

(a) *What do you think the artist is trying to portray?*

PENTECOST

Pentecost is the Christian festival which celebrates the birthday of the church. It is also called Whitsun or 'White Sunday' because of the tradition that people wore white clothes to church on this day. This was because it was a joyful occasion. White also symbolises the purity of God

who is believed to have come to the first disciples at this time in the form of the Holy Spirit.

Whitsun is fifty days after Easter because the first Whitsun happened during the Jewish festival of Pentecost which comes fifty days after Passover, the festival during which Jesus died. The New Testament records the story:

> 'While the day of Pentecost was running its course they were all together in one place, when suddenly there came from the sky a noise like that of a strong driving wind, which filled the whole house where they were sitting. And there appeared to them tongues like flames of fire, dispersed among them and resting on each one. And they were all filled with the Holy Spirit and began to talk in other tongues, as the Spirit gave them power of utterance.' (Acts 2:1-4)

Up until this time Jesus' followers had stayed hidden in Jerusalem. Now that Jesus was no longer with them in a bodily form, they were waiting for God to send them another to guide and support them, as Jesus had promised. At Pentecost they believed that the promise had come true. Suddenly they knew that their job was to preach the Good News about Jesus, and they found within themselves the strength to do it.

How they spoke 'in other tongues' we do not know. Some Christians think they were miraculously blessed with the knowledge of foreign languages; others, that they made themselves understood in the common Greek language of the day. Or perhaps this is an example of 'glossolalia' when normal words and logical sentences cannot contain the flood of emotion which wells up inside someone, so that they have to utter what may sound like gibberish but which Christians describe as the language of the Spirit. Whatever it means, this occasion is recorded as the beginning of the church. It started with the inspired preaching of a small group of people but was destined to become a world-wide movement.

ASSIGNMENTS

4 Describe or draw the story of the first Whitsun.

5 What two things does white symbolise?

Symbols of the Holy Spirit

Christians believe that those first disciples were affected by God the Holy Spirit, and that all Christians can know God in this way. The Holy Spirit is the name used for God when he is felt to be active in the lives of men and women, inspiring all that is good and loving in their lives. Christians believe that the Holy Spirit was the power in the life of Jesus Christ and lives on after him in the men and women who follow in his footsteps.

We shall never know exactly what those disciples really felt at that Pentecost. Feelings are difficult to put into words. But they described the coming of the Holy Spirit to them in the symbols of wind and fire.

(a) Why do people like to gather round bonfires?

Fire is a good symbol for God. We use fire to burn up rubbish, just as God is said to destroy evil by working through people who are prepared

to stand out against what they believe is wrong. Fire is also used to produce energy: the furnace in a ship's engine room needs to be well-stoked if the ship is to move along. Similarly, the Spirit of God is said to inflame people into action. And of course, fire is a source of warmth. Even in this age of central heating, many of us know the comfort of sitting round a glowing fire. In the same way, the Holy Spirit is said to be God's way of warming people to each other, melting cold hearts, and giving people a sense of well-being. There is also something fascinating about a live fire which attracts and holds our gaze. God is said to be like that too, having an almost magnetic pull which draws people to him.

We are told that there was a noise like that of a strong, driving wind. We do not know whether it was a sound that anyone could have heard and which we could have recorded. But what is significant is that the Greek word was the same for both 'wind' and 'spirit' and therefore this was a very good way to symbolise the coming of the Holy Spirit. Jesus himself is recorded in John's Gospel as comparing the two.

Wind is another very good symbol for God's Spirit since there are so many similarities between the two. Like the wind, the Holy Spirit is invisible and yet Christians claim that its activity leaves them in no doubt as to its existence. Like the wind which can blow up very suddenly, so it is said that the Holy Spirit can take people by surprise, working through the most unlikely people at the least expected times. When the wind blows there is little we can do to control it although we can harness its power to drive windmills and sailing ships and so on. Christians say that, in the same way, when God calls people, they can either dig in and wait for the feeling to pass, or they can allow God's Spirit to give them new strength. Like the fierce, cold wind from the North, the Holy Spirit is said to pierce people's conscience and convict them of their sins. Like the warm South winds, it is said to bring people the comfort of God's love.

Another very common symbol for the Holy Spirit is the dove. We have already come across this in the story of Jesus' baptism. The Holy Spirit is portrayed in paintings and sculptures as this gentle, pure white bird. It symbolises the way that God influences people lovingly and gently.

(a)   What invisible force is causing all the havoc here?

(b)   How do you know that it is very powerful?

(c)   How do you think you would have felt if you had been the photographer?

ASSIGNMENTS

6 What do Christians mean when they speak of God the Holy Spirit?

7 Find out what Jesus said about the Spirit and the wind in John 3:8.

8 What did the Holy Spirit do to Jesus' followers at Pentecost which was like the action of the wind?

9 Imagine a huge bonfire at a Guy Fawkes' party. In what ways could this fire be said to symbolise the Holy Spirit?

10 Try to think of a different symbol for the Holy Spirit. Explain the similarities between the thing you have chosen and the Christian idea of God the Holy Spirit.

TRINITY SUNDAY

Pentecost was so important that it has given its name to the rest of the Church's year.

The first Sunday after Pentecost is Trinity Sunday, when Christians are reminded of their distinctive belief in God the Holy Trinity.

The word 'trinity' (tri-unity) means 'three in one'. Christians have never doubted that there is only one God but they say that God has made himself known to them in three different ways: as Father, Son, and Holy Spirit. They say that each is fully and really God, but that we can understand God better if we know all of his three Persons. This is such an important idea that it is expressed in all the Christian Creeds, or statements of belief.

The Christian idea of the Trinity is very difficult to explain and therefore Christians have used symbols to show what they mean. One of the most famous was used by Saint Patrick when he first took Christianity to Ireland. He used the shamrock leaf as his symbol because it has three parts to it and yet it is only one leaf. A similar

modern example is a triangle. This always has three sides and yet is only one triangle.

Another traditional image is that of the sun. The sun is the source of all life on earth, just as God the Father is known as the creator of all things. The sun gives light and God the Son is called the 'Light of the World'. It also gives warmth which cannot be seen but felt. This is like God the Holy Spirit, for Christians say that they can feel him working through them. A similar, modern example is that of an electric fire. The invisible electric power can be compared to God the Father; the light it gives to the Son; and the heat to the Holy Spirit. All are parts of the one fire.

Perhaps the best symbols are those taken from people rather than things, since Christians believe in three Persons of the Trinity. Think of yourself: you have a mind which controls all that you think and do. This is like God the Father who is seen as being in charge. You have a body just as the Son of God appeared in bodily form in the man Jesus. You also have emotions and this part of you can be compared to the Holy Spirit. Again thinking of people, one person could be a grandmother, mother, sister, aunt, cousin and so on. She is all of these people even though she is really only one person. In the same way Christians say that God can be Father, Son and Holy Spirit even though he is really only one God.

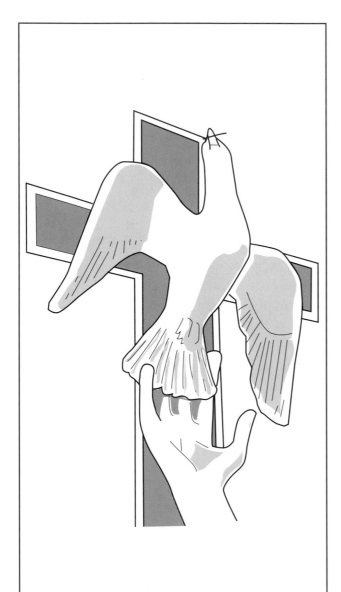

(a) How can you tell that this is a Christian sculpture?

(b) The three parts of this sculpture appear to represent the three-in-one God;

(i) what Person of the Trinity is represented by the Cross?

(ii) whom does the dove symbolise?

(iii) whom could the hand supporting it all stand for?

A SUMMARY

Forty days after Easter, Christians celebrate Ascension Day. They believe that once Jesus had convinced his followers that he was really alive, he returned to his rightful place with God his Father. They say he was taken up into the sky. This puts across the idea that Christ is above us, he is greater than us.

The New Testament says that God did not leave the disciples alone for very long; after Jesus had left them, God began to work through them. We are told that this started at Pentecost, the first Whit Sunday, which is when the church began. The disciples believed that God was giving them inner strength to spread the Good News that Jesus really was the Saviour. They called this inner strength the Holy Spirit of God.

The last half of the church's year is called Pentecost and it starts with Trinity Sunday. During this time the church draws together all the things it has learnt about God. It has learnt that God the Father sent both his Son and the Holy Spirit into the world to help men and women. So Christians believe that although there is only one God, there are three ways of understanding him: as Father, Son and Holy Spirit. This is what trinity means: three-in-one.

SUBJECT INDEX

INDEX OF RELIGIOUS SYMBOLS